Fundraising Advice for College and University Presidents

An Insider's Guide

by Rita Bornstein

Fundraising Advice for College and University Presidents: An Insider's Guide

Library of Congress Cataloging-in-Publication Data

Bornstein, Rita.
   Fundraising advice for college and university presidents : an insider's guide / Rita Bornstein.
       p. cm.
     ISBN 978-0-926508-09-5
1. Educational fund raising--United States. 2. Universities and colleges--United States--Finance. I. Title.
     LB2336.B67 2011
     378.1'06--dc23
                                        2011040768

For more information on AGB Press publications or to order additional copies of this book, call 800/356-6317 or visit the AGB website at www.agb.org.

TABLE OF CONTENTS

Foreword

REGARDLESS OF THE PATHS THEY FOLLOWED on their way to the presidency, chief executive officers of today's colleges and universities are expected to serve as their institutions' lead fundraisers. While fundraising is perhaps not all presidents' preferred responsibility, virtually all institutional constituencies look to their president or chancellor as the primary advocate for private support and investment.

Whether for capital projects or academic initiatives associated with comprehensive campaigns, endowment support, or other areas requiring private funds, donors (especially major gift donors and prospects) and others expect the chief executive to be an effective advocate for private resources to support an institution's funding priorities. Search committees typically make it quite clear that in addition to administrative and academic leadership, they expect their chief executive to lead the overall fundraising effort.

Governing boards typically include fundraising effectiveness as one of the specific areas for which they hold their presidents accountable. The mutual expectations between presidents and boards concerning fundraising leadership make this an especially important attribute for presidents in what is presumed to be a collaborative effort. As AGB's Task Force on The Academic Presidency noted in its 2006 report *The Leadership Imperative*: "At a time when public financial support for higher education has waned relative to other priorities, success in fundraising has taken on elevated significance, and no president or governing board can fail to perceive the importance of this leadership requirement. Presidents whose achievements in other respects may be remarkable will be judged harshly if they cannot also attract substantial private funds to their institutions."

Sophisticated fundraising efforts are equally vital to public institutions, where such efforts are often led by institutionally related foundations, as at independent colleges and universities. And, while fundraising won't substitute for primary revenue sources—tuition, public support and, for some, benefits from endowment earnings—private support is increasingly vital to the revenue requirements of most institutions of higher education. By extension, the need for presidents' consistent and skilled engagement in fundraising is an ever more important part of the job.

In *Fundraising Advice for College and University Presidents: An Insider's Guide*, Rita Bornstein—distinguished president emerita of Rollins College, board member, professor of philanthropy and leadership development, and a former vice president for development—draws on her years of experience and expertise to offer an insider's view of presidential fundraising leadership. Dr. Bornstein explains the various roles of the president, the governing board (or the foundation board in public institutions), the chief development officer, and the development staff in the fundraising process. She offers informed advice on how to cultivate and nourish relationships with prospects—and, of course, how to ask them for money. She clarifies the finer points of annual funds, major gifts, and mega gifts and outlines strategies for securing and administering those funds. She elucidates the reasons that donors give in the first place (and why they don't) and how to steer toward a successful result. And she explains how to develop a focused and inspired campaign, build the right staff to manage it, and ensure its success.

Complete with advice, anecdotes, and lessons learned first-hand, *Fundraising Advice for College and University Presidents: An Insider's Guide* will prove invaluable to college and university presidents as they seek to hone their fundraising skills to help their institutions prosper in these financially challenging times. It also is useful reading for institution board members, especially board officers and members of board development and campaign committees. Moreover, its insights can be helpful not only to higher education leaders, but also those in other nonprofit organizations for which fundraising is a priority.

AGB is pleased to publish Dr. Bornstein's timely and lively guide to succeeding at—and even enjoying—the pursuit of fundraising. We hope that this work helps higher education leaders, development professionals, and others achieve their fundraising goals and obtain the financial support their institutions need to thrive and prosper in the 21st century.

Richard D. Legon
President, AGB
October 2011

Acknowledgments

I AM INDEBTED to Rick Legon, president of AGB, for fighting to publish this book, and to my editors Marla Bobowick, Julie Bourbon, and Ellen Hirzy for their thoughtful and creative advice and assistance. AGB's peer reviewers provided comments and suggestions that enhanced the content and scope of the book, and my friend, the journalist Ann Hellmuth, reminded me of the power of storytelling to convey a message.

I learned about fundraising at the University of Miami working with President Edward T. Foote, Board Chair James W. McLamore, and our campaign consultants James P. Seymour, George A. Brakeley Jr., and George A. Brakeley III. Our fundraising success at Rollins College was in great measure due to the groundwork of my predecessor, Thaddeus Seymour, the leadership and discipline of Vice Presidents Warren Johnson and Anne B. Kerr, the devotion and participation of the board of trustees, and the support of the faculty.

I am grateful to my son, Mark, for suggesting that I write a book about fundraising and for giving me helpful feedback about early drafts. My daughter Rachel, stepson Per, and his wife Anne have been great cheerleaders during the process, and my grandchildren, Ariel, Hayley, Signe, and Ezio, have made me optimistic about the future, when philanthropy will still be an essential aspect of American life.

Rita Bornstein
September 2011

Introduction
Developing Fundraising Confidence

● ●

It is apparent that a successful development effort will be required for your tenure as president to be a success, and if you do not enjoy that part of the job, you are well advised to decline the offer. . . . The chief fundraiser is the president.[1]

Peter T. Flawn, President Emeritus, University of Texas at Austin

ALTHOUGH PHILANTHROPY HAS LONG PLAYED a vital role in shaping American higher education, even in the early days, some presidents were ambivalent about fundraising. In 1847, the president of Randolph Macon College wrote to his wife, "This is the least agreeable of all my functions—the begging part, I mean."[2] Today, both public and independent college and university presidents are evaluated in part on their success in fundraising, even though many still consider the process disagreeable.

In the 21st century, the importance of philanthropy continues to grow as the cost of providing higher education escalates and government funding diminishes as a percentage of institutional budgets, especially in the public sector. Yet just about every president, at different times in his or her career, has one or more of the following fears about fundraising:

- I will not be able to ask for money.
- The prospect will decline my request for support.
- I will be perceived as a corporate executive instead of an academic leader.
- I will ask for the wrong amount or the wrong project at the wrong time.
- I will be fired if I don't raise money.

This book, written especially for university and college presidents, is also applicable to the work of all nonprofit CEOs. It is intended to demystify fundraising, make a case for board involvement, and provide tips for success—and to help presidents overcome the idea that asking for money is undignified, demeaning, or in any way like begging. It is based on the triumphs and failures that I experienced or witnessed in more than two decades of higher education fundraising and the consulting I have done with other colleges and universities.

When I was elected president of Rollins College in 1990, I was a nontraditional choice since I did not come through the usual academic route. I was serving as vice president for development at the University of Miami, where I had led a campaign that raised more than $517 million. Campaigns have grown much larger since the 1980s, but that was one of the largest in the country at the time.

In the early 1990s the country was experiencing a serious recession, the college budget was tight, we had to undertake large-scale layoffs, and we were undistinguished in national rankings. In that inauspicious context, I began meeting people, soliciting annual fund gifts, getting control of spending, and slowly improving quality in every part of the college, from landscaping to admission standards.

As an underendowed college with great aspirations, Rollins needed a president who would be an aggressive fundraiser. I was ready for a presidency but knew my background would be an impediment to acceptance among certain constituents. At first, the reception was mixed. Some board members and alumni thought I could not possibly connect with the college's constituents. Some faculty members wanted to use me as their personal development officer, others thought I was too corporate, and still others kept asking when I was going to start bringing in the big dollars.

Any new president needs perseverance, but I had to prove my ability to serve as a president of whom all constituents could be proud. I had to learn to not be self-conscious about my background in fundraising and to see success in that area as vital to institutional improvement and repositioning. One of my early goals was to develop strong relationships with faculty members, students, parents, board members, alumni, and business and community leaders.

Coupled with my emphasis on quality throughout the institution was our planning and execution of an unprecedented fundraising campaign. When I began floating a goal of $100 million, many board members were nervous and skeptical. The largest campaign the college had ever conducted brought in close to $44 million. But the board recognized that it had hired an experienced fundraiser as president, and although some members stepped down during the planning period, most were willing to follow my lead.

It turned out that Rollins was the perfect match for my talents and interests. I was attracted to its beautiful campus, location in an urban area, sophisticated faculty, fascinating history of educational innovation, loyal alumni, and committed board of trustees. I put together a strong administration, involved the faculty, and strengthened the board. Together, we gathered the resources and transformed the college.

During my 14 years as president, we strengthened the college's fiscal health, academic quality, and national reputation. We raised more than $160 million through the campaign and secured a significant bequest from an alumnus. We built or renovated numerous facilities, bought much-needed properties, added many endowed chairs, invested in new programs, and enhanced student financial-aid funds. I became active in higher education associations to help bring Rollins to national prominence.

Not all development leaders can become successful presidents, but all presidents must become successful fundraisers. Today, this requirement is written into most job descriptions for presidents of both public and independent institutions. Some come to their new positions from a different type of institution—smaller or larger, public or independent, denominational or nondenominational. They may have been deans or vice presidents and had little fundraising experience, or they may have come to the post from outside of higher education. Whatever the president's background, the art of fundraising can be learned, and it can be fun.

Unfortunately, according to a survey conducted by the *Chronicle of Higher Education*, many presidents are unprepared for this part of the job—and this is likely still the trend today. Eighty-seven percent of the survey respondents said they were either "very well prepared" or "moderately well prepared" to serve as president. But when asked, "What were you most unprepared for in your current job as president?" the most frequent response (18 percent) was fundraising, even though 53 percent said they engaged in fundraising on a daily basis.[3]

The practical advice in the following chapters encourages presidents to explore, embrace, and enjoy fundraising. This book is not a "how-to" manual that covers all aspects of managing a development operation, nor is it a guide to running an annual fund or a capital campaign or for setting up a planned giving office. Instead, it is a president's perspective on the fundraising process, with tips for success and issues to consider. It is organized around the premise that a president has eight essential tasks in fundraising:

1. Develop a vision and plan that integrate fundraising.
2. Engage the board.
3. Work with the development staff.
4. Cultivate relationships.

> **A presidential tenure often is judged by the incumbent's legacy of fundraising as much as or more than by improvements in student recruitment and retention, academic quality, or faculty credentials.**

5. Organize an infrastructure for fundraising.

6. Ask for money.

7. Develop and lead fundraising campaigns.

8. Accept, decline, and manage gifts.

Given the financial challenges that confront our institutions today, fundraising will continue to be a key component of a president's portfolio. In a down economy, the challenges are to maintain and increase fundraising revenue and attract and retain experienced fundraising staff. Presidents need to be actively engaged in cultivating relationships, asking for money, and helping people understand the connection between mission and money. It is important to remember that a presidential tenure often is judged by the incumbent's legacy of fundraising as much as or more than by improvements in student recruitment and retention, academic quality, or faculty credentials.

Many presidents—sometimes to their surprise—find that fundraising is not onerous but interesting, an opportunity to blend their strengths in intellectual leadership with their capacity to meet financial challenges by aggressively stimulating philanthropy.

Chapter 1
Integrating Vision and Fundraising

● ●

A president can induce change by introducing resources…. Presidents leave their mark on an institution by their ability to inspire innovation, and that has to do with their ability to pay for it.[4]

Stephen Joel Trachtenberg, President Emeritus, George Washington University

BOARD MEMBERS, FACULTY MEMBERS, ALUMNI, AND STUDENTS are always eager to know what their president's vision is for the institution. Effective presidents draw on the hopes and dreams of constituents to develop a vision and, in collaboration with these groups, formulate strategic plans and identify critical needs. A vision should be aspirational and state, in bold language, how institutional leaders see the future. It should generate hope and excitement and mobilize the support of constituents. It should be based on an institution's history and ambitions and establish a general direction for change. Although the vision and mission of a public institution are often more targeted to meeting a state's agenda, the presi-

Vision, mission, and money are intertwined. Fulfilling a vision and mission is not possible without resources, and raising money is challenging without an exciting vision and mission.

dent still has a chance to shape the institution within that context.

Most presidents share their vision, mission, and strategy in public for the first time at their formal inaugurations. At that moment, all things seem possible, all goals attainable. Then reality sets in. Where will the resources come from to achieve the vision? Endowment? Budgeting? Enrollment? Borrowing? State funding? Philanthropy? All of these sources can be helpful, but every board and faculty expects their president to help fulfill the institution's promise through philanthropy. The bottom line is that vision, mission, and money are intertwined. Fulfilling a vision and mission is not possible without resources, and raising money is challenging without an exciting vision and mission.

When I interviewed for the Rollins College presidency, I was asked about my vision for the place, and so I began to develop and articulate one. I had prepared by studying the college's history, strategic plans, mission statements, and news stories. I talked with board members, faculty members, and community leaders. My vision for Rollins was national recognition as one of America's best colleges. I emphasized the values of excellence, innovation, and community.

After I became president, I made it a priority to include all constituents in amplifying and refining this vision. I knew that presidents who try to impose a vision are frequently rebuffed. Stakeholders must feel that the institutional vision includes their perspectives before they can rally around it. First, I established and chaired the Task Force on the 21st Century, which drafted vision and mission statements, goals, and objectives. Then the task force convened an all-day, all-college planning summit to review and discuss these documents. Revisions were made, and relevant sections were sent to faculty and board-governance bodies for approval. One important outcome of this process was achieving consensus on another goal: to make Rollins the number-one college choice for significantly more students. I was open to dialogue and change, and I believe we developed a stronger and broader collegial commitment because everyone "owned" the vision for the college's future.

Perhaps the most challenging issue was reconciling the college's historic and cultural commitment to both the traditional liberal arts and an applied, pragmatic, Deweyan educational philosophy. Using language and concepts that integrated these traditions—"Rollins is committed to a pragmatic, liberal education, applying learning to the solution of social problems"—enabled constituents to unite behind the vision.

Fundraising as Relational and Integral

It is not uncommon for presidents to compartmentalize their responsibilities: "Today, I am wearing my fundraising hat," or "Today, I am wearing my lobbying hat." Instead of a series of hats, it is helpful to imagine one big hat under which many different activities occur at the same time. Fundraising is integrally connected with the president's academic, student, financial, and community activities.

Presidents must invest considerable time in nurturing and developing relationships, and no one can take their place in this process. When people lose confidence in a president, or feel they have lost their connection to him or her, they turn their philanthropic interests elsewhere. The urgency of fundraising requires that presidents spend considerable time off campus developing those relationships, communicating the institutional vision, and soliciting support. This process becomes easier over time.

When Frank H. T. Rhodes was president of Cornell University, he demonstrated an amazing ability to befriend the institution's constituents and engage them in fulfilling his vision. Still, faculty members often criticized him for spending so much time off campus. Stephen Joel Trachtenberg raised millions of dollars as president of George Washington University. He points out that the faculty may

A high level of board participation in fundraising sends a positive message to constituents about the board's commitment to the institution.

....

expected to contribute to the annual fund and to make stretch gifts to campaigns. A high level of board participation in fundraising sends a positive message to constituents about the board's commitment to the institution. Because board members are insiders, their financial investments reflect their confidence in the college or university and its leadership, thus setting an example for others. Board members can also support the fundraising operation by identifying prospects, providing prospect information, making introductions, hosting events, and making solicitations.

Many board members are poorly prepared to accept these responsibilities. Research and observation indicate that they find expectations for fundraising unrealistic, although it is one of the areas they report spending the most time on. Board members, like presidents, come to enjoy fundraising the more they engage in it and the more success they have.

When I arrived at Rollins, I was determined to enlist the board in fundraising. A few board members were experienced in fundraising for other nonprofits and were of tremendous help in promoting a philanthropic mindset. We made fundraising one of the first items on our board-meeting agendas; discussed the strategy and policy that would be consistent with our vision, mission, and strategic planning; and reinforced the board's role. I reported on our campaign goals and achievements at every meeting, and we often took the board on a tour of new facilities. Some board members became excellent solicitors; some hosted events in their homes or one-on-one meetings in their clubs. Board members reviewed endless lists of prospects, and many contributed valuable insights and information.

The President's Educational Role

The president has a major role in underscoring the importance of board involvement in fundraising and explaining how vital its leadership and involvement are to the process. The board may not give enough attention to its responsibility for oversight of the fundraising operation because most board members, in my observation and in conversation with other presidents, prefer serving on athletics, facilities, finance, and investment committees. They may prefer to leave fundraising to the president and development staff. They often say that they will do just about anything for the institution—except ask for money. They may not have been educated on ways they can help, or they may not have had good fundraising experiences.

It helps to view fundraising in the context of the proud tradition of philanthropy in American life and in higher education. No other country has the commitment to philanthropy and volunteerism that is part of our national character and culture. Without philanthropy, our great educational and medical institutions might not exist or serve as world leaders in their fields. Without philanthropy, we might not have the diverse organizations that serve the variety of American interests. Without philanthropy, we might not have made such extraordinary progress in fighting disease, developing scientific inventions, or providing a broad array of education, culture, and health-care programs.

The president, working with the board chair, can strengthen the board's interest in and commitment to development by rotating people on committees, making the topic an agenda priority, and devoting time to working with the board on

We made fundraising one of the first items on our board meeting agendas; discussed the strategy and policy that would be consistent with our vision, mission, and strategic planning; and reinforced the board's role.

development strategy. The planning and execution of a campaign generally elicit excitement among board members when they realize the impact of fundraising on the institutional vision and mission. Development becomes more interesting when there is an emphasis on strategy, policy, and performance. At one midsized university, a board member who appreciated the president's desire to improve retention provided the funds to purchase a three-story apartment building adjacent to campus and convert it to a residence hall for upper-division students. This desirable location kept these students on campus and promoted a spirit of community. The donor's gift was an excellent example of the interconnection of mission and money.

What Board Members Can Do

Since fundraising is one of the most important board responsibilities, the president and chief development officer, with the board chair's guidance, need to provide training on just what board members are being asked to do and how. When board members and presidents work together, the institution is more likely to fulfill its fundraising potential.

A strong board builds fundraising into the job description for board members and makes it part of the annual assessment of the president and the board. Board leaders and the president should be clear and frank about individual board members' responsibilities for making personal contributions and assisting with fundraising. Explain and reinforce these expectations often: before an individual agrees to join the board, at board orientation sessions, at regular board meetings, at special sessions or board retreats guided by consultants, and at board-member evaluations.

Periodically, board members should be asked to review lists of prospective donors to identify people they may know and with whom they might be helpful. They can also identify people and organizations that have not been involved in the institution's work but may become interested. They can set up meetings for the president, host social gatherings, and provide useful information to help cultivate prospects. They can accompany the president on get-acquainted visits and solicitations. Reluctant board members do not necessarily have to ask for money, but their presence adds gravitas. As participants in a solicitation meeting, they can testify to the quality of a project and their own interest and involvement.

One board member I know accompanied the president on a solicitation call. As the meeting went on, he thought that the president would never get to the point. The board member had to get back to his office, so at a pause in the conversation he jumped in and made the request. The prospect's response was quick and positive. As a result of this experience, the board member became much more enthusiastic about fundraising.

There are, of course, board members who will not participate in the fundraising process. Some of them substitute generous personal giving, but others neither give money nor provide assistance. This matter should be addressed in annual evaluations of board members' contributions and also by the committee on trustees. Board members who are not contributing to the health and welfare of the institution may be asked to rotate off the board.

Board Members as Advocates

Fundraising success depends in great measure on an institution's reputation, and board advocacy can help. Board members have a special role as advocates for their

Five Ways Board Members Can Get Involved in Fundraising

1. Give generously to the annual fund and to comprehensive campaigns, setting an example for others.
2. Review prospect lists and provide information about capacity and appropriate solicitors.
3. Connect the president and chief development officer with prospects.
4. Participate in solicitations.
5. Communicate appreciation to major donors.

As board members gain experience in their roles, they will internalize the vision, mission, and goals of the institution and become clear and convincing advocates.

institutions and for higher education. They are insiders who can speak knowledgably about the institution they serve. They are generally well-respected, high-status people who have many contacts and are peers of prospective donors. Often, they are active and visible in their communities or even on a national scale. As board members gain experience in their roles, they will internalize the vision, mission, and goals of the institution and become clear and convincing advocates. The administration can periodically prepare board members by providing a brief written overview of the institution's mission, achievements, and needs. It is always appropriate to include mention of the institution's fundraising goals and progress toward them. It is also helpful if board members can talk knowledgeably about the challenges and contributions of higher education in general.

Frequently, people from outside the institution ask a board member how things are going. The board member needs to be able to respond comfortably with an "elevator speech"—a few comments that cover goals, accomplishments, and fundraising activities: "I am so pleased you asked. The university is on a roll. We have raised our admission standards and our graduation rates. We have improved our national rankings. Our ambitious $250 million campaign has brought in $182 million so far. We've built six new facilities in the last six years, endowed faculty chairs so we can hire and retain the best, and increased financial aid to help us recruit the students we want. I would enjoy sharing more information about our progress. Why don't you come to the president's presentation at the Chamber of Commerce tomorrow at noon?"

Fundraising at Public Institutions

Historically, boards of public institutions were rarely expected to engage in much fundraising or even to contribute generous financial support. Since the 1970s, however, state support has declined as a percentage of institutions' revenue, and private support has grown in importance. At most public institutions, presidents are now expected to play an active leadership role in fundraising, and increasingly they are evaluated on their effectiveness in that capacity. Some states are committed to providing matching funds for private-sector gifts, a great spur to philanthropy. It is no longer true that individuals are reluctant to give to public institutions because they are supported in part by tax dollars. As a result, public and private institutions are in direct competition for philanthropic support.

At approximately half of all public institutions, affiliated foundations, set up as separate 501(c)(3) charitable corporations, are responsible for oversight and execution of fundraising on behalf of the institution. Foundation boards traditionally have been more active than governing boards in fundraising. According to research conducted by AGB in 2010, 59 percent of public institutions reported that 80 percent or more of the members of their governing board had made a contribution in the past year. In comparison, 82 percent of foundations reported that 80 percent or more of the board had made contributions in the past year, and that foundation-board giving accounted for an average of 18 percent of all individual gifts to public institutions. As state support for public higher education continues to decline and private support is more crucial for funding student financial aid and faculty positions, institution boards will need to assume greater fundraising responsibility.

Foundation boards [in public institutions] can ... be instrumental in helping institution leaders identify projects that are likely to attract private support.

Working with the president and other academic leaders, public governing boards are responsible for identifying fundraising priorities. Foundation boards can, however, be instrumental in helping institution leaders identify projects that are likely to attract private support. While the organization and oversight of fundraising varies widely among public institutions, many foundations, especially at larger universities, are partially or fully responsible for fundraising oversight and execution and are a significant source of financial support for development functions. Foundations also have a major part in campaign planning and leadership, helping to develop case statements, setting campaign goals, identifying staffing and other resources, and monitoring campaign progress.

Good relations and communications between governing and foundation boards are vital to successful fundraising. These relationships can be enhanced, when possible, by having some governing-board members serve on the foundation board or its committees; conducting joint meetings or retreats; and holding regular meetings of the president, foundation chief executive, and governing- and foundation-board chairs. This approach enhances the prestige of the foundation board and its development-related committees. If one or two high-stature governing board members agree to serve, others may be encouraged to participate. Collaboration among institution and foundation leaders also signals the importance of fundraising and can enhance the effectiveness of institutional advocacy efforts. Collaboration and coordination in both fundraising and advocacy are especially important in multicampus and system institutions to ensure that major-gift prospects are not receiving multiple requests for support, and that legislators and prospective donors hear a unified message about institutional priorities.

TIPS FOR PRESIDENTS

- **Educate the board about fundraising roles and expectations.** Few board members look forward to raising money, but the task is less onerous—and even rewarding—when they understand the many contributions they can make, from brainstorming prospective donors, to hosting events, to joining you on prospect visits or making solicitations.

- **Remind board members that giving comes before asking.** Be explicit about the importance of individual giving from board members, and let them know that full board participation sets an essential example for others to follow.

- **Get to know board members individually.** These relationships can link you to prospective donors, generate specific ideas for fundraising strategy, and give you a sense of board members' interests and capabilities. And when you match members with meaningful assignments that use their experience, talents, and contacts, overall board performance benefits.

- **Give board members the knowledge and support they need to succeed at fundraising.** Start with focused training on fundraising goals, needs, strategies, and techniques. Expose them to research on fundraising trends and results in higher education. Ensure that the chief development officer reports regularly on fundraising results.

- **Keep the board in the loop.** Follow through and report on their suggestions about prospects. Thank them publicly and often for their involvement in the fundraising effort and their monetary contributions to the institution.

Chapter 3
Working with the Development Staff

● ●

A president ... has the ability to influence the spirits of the fundraising staff and the volunteers, as it helps the effort enormously if both groups enjoy the challenges provided by a campaign and have some fun working together.[7]

Mary Patterson McPherson, President Emeritus, Bryn Mawr College

SOME PRESIDENTS MAY NOT FULLY APPRECIATE that fundraisers are skilled professionals with specialized expertise. They may believe that anyone can raise money, even if they feel insecure about their own ability to do so. Presidents who treat the discussion of money as dirty business unworthy of their time may prefer to leave fundraising to the development staff. Such a lack of fundraising leadership may lead to lost opportunities for major gifts, unfulfilled needs, staff resignations, and disarray in the development office. On the other hand, presidents who embrace fundraising as a part of their portfolios will create strong relationships with the development team, and especially with the chief development officer. A close rapport based on trust, mutual respect, and reciprocity is necessary for a president to be successful at fundraising.

The relationship of the president and chief development officer is so vital that it deserves a lot of attention. A national survey of chief development officers found that "for the president and CDO to work effectively together, it is critical for each to understand the roles and responsibilities of the other." A lack of "role clarity" leads to misunderstanding and uncertainty.[8]

When I was vice president for development at the University of Miami, I had a close working relationship with the president and the board chair. During our campaign, we met weekly with our consultant to review progress and plan next steps. At Rollins, I found a similar close relationship between my predecessor and the development vice president. This situation seemed to bode well, but I quickly found that the vice president was intimidated by my development experience. I knew too much about his work for him to feel comfortable. My approach was to let him take the initiative and to follow his lead, because he knew the college and the prospects. I knew the importance of building relationships, preparing for prospect meetings carefully, and debriefing with the vice president. During the quiet phase of our big campaign, working closely together, he and I secured a very large gift. Making sure there were no observers, we danced happily around my office.

Although we worked well together, sometimes our relationship was prickly. I had

Presidents who embrace fundraising as a part of their portfolios will create strong relationships with the development team, especially the chief development officer.

> **The chief development officer positions the president as the institution's legitimate leader, committed to the students and dedicated to fulfilling the mission.**

high expectations for the development operation and was easily disappointed. When the vice president retired, I hired the development officer from the Crummer Graduate School of Business at Rollins. Over the years, I had found her to be indefatigable, knowledgable, and a terrific relationship builder. We admired, respected, and trusted each other. After she became vice president we raised a lot of money together. She took all she learned and has applied it successfully to her own college presidency.

The Chief Development Officer's Responsibilities

Chief development officers (CDOs) owe their presidents good research, thorough briefings, and judicious use of their time. It is up to the CDO to position the president as the institution's legitimate leader, committed to the students and dedicated to fulfilling the mission.

The CDO also prepares the president to become a good fundraiser by working to ensure early success in the process. This means approaching first those prospects who are closest to the institution and ready to make a contribution. Before the president makes a solicitation, the CDO should lay the groundwork that will lead to an affirmative response. With rare exceptions, a president who has faith in the expertise of the CDO needs to accept her or his recommendations for interactions with prospects. On the other hand, presidents must discuss with their CDOs any reservations they have about proposed fundraising activities, including cultivation events and solicitations. Finally, the CDO can weed out unnecessary invitations, determine which events to delegate to others, and help the president decide which events are essential, how long to stay, and whether the spouse must attend. (The spouse's role is often a sensitive subject. My husband was pleased to participate in the range of activities I attended, but after the first few years, he was also happy to be excused from certain events.)

The chief development officer also establishes, explains, and evaluates fundraising goals and keeps governing and foundation boards informed through comprehensive reports. Board members need to have at their disposal such metrics as the costs of fundraising, staff productivity, and year-to-year fundraising comparisons, as well as carefully assembled data from comparable institutions. Benchmarking data are available from the Council for Advancement and Support of Education (CASE).

Monthly contact reports by staff are also an excellent management tool for the CDO. At an independent institution, the CDO's connection with the board is primarily through the development committee. At a public institution, the CDO may be the president of the foundation. In advance of meetings, the CDO should review the development agenda with the committee chair or foundation president, as appropriate. The caveat is "no surprises." If there is bad news—goals not met, excessive staff turnover, insufficient resources to fund campaign materials—the CDO should discuss the problem with the president and committee or foundation chair in advance of the meeting.

The chief development officer, with the support of the president, board, and committee chairs, is also responsible for educating the board about its fundraising responsibilities. This can be done with the help of a consultant, if necessary. Every six months to a year, the CDO should visit with each board member individually to seek assistance with identifying, cultivating, and soliciting prospects.

It is up to the chief development officer to assemble a capable, high-performing development staff with the professional and personal qualities that support fundraising success. Professional staff members should enjoy interacting with a wide range of people, and they should be interesting, well read, and aware of current issues.

Adequate staffing is just as important as staff effectiveness. Each development area—annual fund, major gifts, planned giving, and so on—needs enough

> **Adequate staffing is just as important as staff effectiveness. Each development area—annual fund, major gifts, planned giving, and so on—needs enough staff to ensure regular contact with donors and prospects.**

staff members to ensure regular contact with donors and prospects. If the staff is stretched too thin and the type, size, and number of gifts are affected, the president should consider a larger investment in the development operation to stimulate a greater philanthropic return. If the development operation is floundering, it is wise to evaluate and perhaps rethink its organization and staffing. An outside consultant or CDO from another institution can help with this internal assessment process.

One of the most important staffing decisions a president makes is the retention or selection of a chief development officer. In a tight economy it is more difficult to find an experienced, eager, and socially adroit CDO; new presidents who come from outside the institution and community would do well to retain the current CDO, if there is one, to take advantage of her or his knowledge of prospects, board members, and fundraising history. When hiring a new CDO, it is important to take time to check references and accomplishments thoroughly and to determine which candidate has a strong connection and shares the same perspective with the president. If a person is a good fit for the institution and appealing to the president, he or she will very likely be appealing to prospects and donors. Even good development staff members are hard to find and retain. Increasingly, institutions are following the prescription to "grow your own."

The President's Responsibilities

In fruitful relationships, presidents accept their reciprocal responsibilities to the chief development officer: making time for prospect review and planning, preparing for cultivation and solicitation meetings, providing thorough debriefings, and discussing general advancement issues. The president must be willing to tell and retell the institutional story to inspire the board, faculty, alumni, students, community leaders, and development staff. When presidents brush aside fundraising activities, they are not doing their jobs. On the other hand, presidents who will not take some direction and advice from the CDO cannot expect to succeed. The president must hold the CDO accountable for results and should expect regular reports on progress toward annual and campaign fundraising goals within previously agreed upon costs and staffing constraints. Presidents need to be sensitive to the stress that the annual fund in particular creates for the chief development officer and other staff, especially at three times of the year:

- During annual budget negotiations, when the president and chief financial officer seek to increase the annual fund goal to help balance the budget while the chief development officer works to keep the goal achievable;
- In the last months of each calendar year, when donors are considering their tax situations and the possibility exists for additional giving; and
- At the end of the academic year, when development officers are scrambling to achieve the annual fund goal.

Both the president and the chief development officer must demonstrate a powerful dedication to strengthening their institution. Their attitudes toward the institution and toward each other send a message to board members and faculty members, who in turn mirror those attitudes. If the president-CDO relationship cannot be made to work, the president needs to find a new development leader. The level of mutual respect, honest feedback, and support must be exceptionally high for the development operation to run smoothly and effectively.

TIPS

FOR PRESIDENTS

The level of mutual respect, honest feedback, and support [between the president and the chief development officer] must be exceptionally high for the development operation to run smoothly and effectively.

- **Publicly acknowledge the good work of the chief development officer and development staff members.** By thanking them for their efforts, you show your support and generate appreciation and respect from others.

- **Drop by the development office occasionally to talk informally with staff members.** Attend a development meeting to announce a new gift and thank the staff for their contributions. Remember that these staff members are also your constituents. They will thrive knowing that you recognize their hard work on behalf of the institution.

- **When appropriate, invite the chief development officer to announce a gift.** The president usually announces big gifts, as this makes her or him look successful. A generous and enlightened president will occasionally invite the CDO to announce a gift, thus sharing the sense of success.

- **Encourage administrators and faculty members to treat development officers with respect.** Constituents emulate the president's attitudes toward development staff. If presidents evince respect and admiration, others will behave in the same way. It is wise to create a sense of shared involvement.

Chapter 4
Cultivating
Relationships

● ●

Many presidents discover to their astonishment that they enjoy raising money. If they have come from academic life, it is a route to meeting new kinds of people and escaping the loneliness on campus, even making new friends.[9]

Arthur Levine, President Emeritus, Teachers College, Columbia University

"CULTIVATION" IS AN APT METAPHOR IN FUNDRAISING. To build relationships with prospective donors, you must plant, fertilize, weed, and harvest—just as in cultivating a garden. By planting the seeds of interest and respect in potential supporters, you expose them to the institution's programs and people, fertilizing their interest with repeated involvement. The goal is to help prospects identify with the institutional mission. If you do not capture their interest after considerable cultivation, you weed them out of your garden. If you do, the fruits of your efforts can be harvested in the form of philanthropy: Once a prospect is brought into the life of the university or college, it becomes appropriate to invite him or her to contribute to its goals.

Cultivation is, ultimately, a highly personal activity. There is no substitute for

As you build relationships with prospective donors, you plant, fertilize, weed, and harvest—just as in cultivating a garden.

the careful cultivation of interest and support, even among those already involved with the institution. Alumni need to be reacquainted with their alma mater as it is today, and board members should be cultivated as important prospects, not taken for granted. There are many opportunities for cultivation: athletic events, theater and music performances, art exhibits, donor-recognition socials, one-on-one meals and visits, and so forth. Presidential participation is not always necessary, unless major prospects are in attendance.

All the while, the development office should be employing a process known as "moves management" to track the interactions of every prospect with representatives of the institution and develop plans for further contact. That process can bring prospects closer to the institution.

From the time I arrived at Rollins, I worked hard at cultivating relationships with prospective donors, but it took time for constituents to view me as their president. In time, I became "the president," and not the woman president, the Jewish president, or the fundraising president. When that time came, I was ready to launch our ambitious campaign, and my cultivation efforts were rewarded. Many people were pleased to support my vision and goals, but of course I found, as all presidents do, that not everyone responded positively to me. Some prospects were strongly connected with the college through a previous president, board member, or faculty member. I was happy to relinquish those prospects to someone who could and would manage the relationships.

Cultivation is a long-term effort and needs to be managed thoughtfully. Large gifts in particular require a significant investment of time and effort. Some years can elapse between the initial conversation and the commitment. One president, for example, approached a former donor several times for support for an important athletic facility. The prospect was friendly but noncommittal. After several years with no progress, the prospect's adult children, alumni of the university, invited the president and his wife to stay with them in their vacation home, near where the prospect also lived for part of the year. This opportunity for informal interaction made the difference, and the next time the president asked for support, the answer was yes. The prospect's son also made a significant contribution to the project.

It Takes a Village

The expression "It takes a village" is appropriate for fundraising, because many people generally are involved: the board member who mentions an acquaintance as a potential prospect, the researcher who gathers intelligence about the prospect's capacity and interests, the development officer who makes the initial contact and determines the prospect's readiness, the faculty member who visits the prospect when traveling in the area, the student who gives the prospect a personalized tour of the campus, the staff member who arranges the cultivation activities, and the vice president who accompanies the president on the solicitation call.

The more people working on identifying, cultivating, and soliciting prospects, the greater the chances of securing increased annual, capital, endowment, and

The more people working on identifying, cultivating, and soliciting prospects, the greater the chances of securing increased annual, capital, endowment, and planned gifts. While the president must be the primary solicitor of major donors, others do much of the work leading up to that point, including former presidents, board members, and development officers.

planned gifts. While the president must be the primary solicitor of major donors, others do much of the work leading up to that point, including former presidents, board members, and development officers.

Administrators and faculty members can be productive "gardeners" in the cultivation and solicitation process. Vice presidents, deans, and directors, for example, often articulate the institution's needs with great passion and clarity. The chief development officer can assign administrators appropriate prospects and support their efforts. Faculty members may know more about their graduates than anyone else. Often, they can identify the alumni who come from wealthy families, their current involvements, classmates with whom they are friendly, and their feelings about the institution. Administrators and faculty members can also be very helpful by accompanying a volunteer to a prospect meeting. Some are especially comfortable around prospects and have excellent presentation skills.

Some administrators and faculty members form relationships with community leaders and other potential prospects by being involved on boards or as members of local organizations. Such organizations can also provide venues for the president or a board member to speak about the institution and its goals and needs. One academic vice president I know was very involved on the local symphony board. He was asked to introduce some of his symphony associates to the university's musical productions. Some were invited to dinner with the president before a concert. In time, the vice president and president were able to interest a few of those symphony supporters in funding music programs at the university.

In addition to serving as "gardeners" who can help cultivate philanthropy, faculty members should be seen as potential contributors. Securing faculty gifts—to the annual fund and to campaigns through outright or planned gifts—can be a challenge. Often faculty members are (or perceive themselves to be) undercompensated. But their dedication to the institution's well-being can spur their philanthropy. Faculty members should be encouraged to participate in the annual fund. A few will make major gifts, most often in the form of a planned gift. Many colleges and universities have benefited from the deep connection felt by a professor who has spent most of his or her professional life at that institution.

The faculty may also support and promote student fundraising projects, generally conducted by the junior and/or senior classes. Encouraging a class to select and fund a project on campus is a good way to emphasize the need for their continuing support and is an important precedent to set: Statistically, students who participate in a class gift while still in school are more likely to support the institution as alumni. Alumni and parents are also good sources of information about prospects and can be helpful in setting up meetings. They can be approached through their associations and boards or when the president is speaking at events.

Both public and independent institutions have a variety of volunteers through their advisory boards, support groups, and foundations. The work of these groups requires coordination to avoid multiple approaches to prospects by enthusiastic

---

The Village at Work

With patience and perseverance, a savvy development officer can mobilize the institutional "village," including the president and other colleagues, to develop and nurture relationships with potentially important prospects.

A university president with a reputation for being one of the nation's top fundraisers began to call on a prospect who had a tenuous relationship with his institution. The prospect's childhood home was located near the university, and a distant relative had supported the institution generously. The prospect himself was an alumnus of a small college near his current residence and served on its board.

Though the connection was not strong,

the university president—knowing of this individual's great financial capacity—visited whenever he was in the area and encouraged faculty members and deans to visit as well. The man and his wife were flattered by the attention of this nationally known, charismatic president and were happy to receive him and his colleagues.

The president's attentiveness and persistence paid off. After a few years, the university president secured several large gifts, including an endowed chair. The donor and his wife left the greatest share of their considerable estate to his alma mater, but they designated a significant gift to the university.

members. However, these membership organizations can provide powerful leverage with community leaders and potential donors.

The Value of Prospect Research

The more presidents know about the finances, family, work, and interests of prospects, the more likely they are to ask for the right amount of support for the right project at the right time. Data-based resources can generate a tremendous amount of information, but they do not provide the personal insights that are gleaned mainly through conversation with prospects and those who know them. These walking-around conversations can yield invaluable clues to a prospect's interests based on chance remarks like, "I loved English," "I was involved in club sports," or "I never set foot in the library." In the survey of chief development officers mentioned in Chapter 3, however, only 40 percent of the respondents indicated that the president played a positive or very positive role in gathering information from prospects and donors. Only 15 percent believed that the president was very good at sharing this critical information with others.[10]

Unfortunately, presidents and volunteers often fail to ensure that these comments and anecdotes find their way into the research files. After an event or a meeting with a prospect, the president needs to debrief with the chief development officer or send an e-mail to the development research staff to make sure all relevant prospect information has been captured. Presidents should also ensure that the research office has up-to-date resources and sufficient staff. The better

The more presidents know about the finances, family, work, and interests of prospects, the more likely they are to ask for the right amount of support for the right project at the right time.

Conversation with prospects and those who know them can yield invaluable clues to a prospect's interests based on chance remarks like, "I loved English," "I was involved in club sports," or "I never set foot in the library."

the background material that solicitors have, the more successful they will be at fundraising.

Cultivation Through Stewardship

Current and former donors are an institution's best prospects, but they cannot be taken for granted. These relationships must be maintained and nurtured through regular contact. Donors appreciate formal recognition and frequent, sincere expressions of gratitude. One board member I know contrasts two colleges he supports: One keeps him apprised of the performance of the projects he has funded and reaches out to him in many ways; the other neglects him entirely even though he has established a generous and irrevocable trust for its benefit. It is not hard to figure out where his primary allegiance lies.

Donors also welcome annual reports that tell them how the endowment is performing and how their funds have been used. Scholarship donors enjoy meeting with recipients and receiving letters from them. Nevertheless, some institutions drop donors from the cultivation cycle once they have made their commitments, or cease contact with prospects not ready to make a gift. Neither habit is smart. Past donors need to be cultivated as potential prospects, and those who say "no" today may say "yes" tomorrow. Good stewardship is the key to future fundraising success.

Although the development office manages stewardship and orchestrates the continuing relationship between donors and the institution, the president has an important role to play. From time to time, a development professional will suggest that the president send a birthday card, write a congratulatory or a condolence note, make a phone call, or extend an invitation to a donor. The president can seek a donor's advice on an issue or request the loan of an art collection for a college museum exhibition. These small acts make a big difference in sustaining connections with donors.

When donors are neglected, they revise their wills to benefit other organizations that interest them. Many presidents tell stories about the bequests that got away. At one institution, as a president retired and another took office, a number of planned giving donors were ignored. By the time the new president and development office became interested, several retirees had taken the institution out of their wills.

Current donors need regular attention and a feeling of involvement, but presidents and board members can go too far in expressions of gratitude. It is not appropriate, for example, to award honorary doctoral degrees to promising prospects or big donors who do not fulfill the usual requirements for the honor. Recipients should set an example for students through their stellar character and impressive record of achievement. Although some philanthropists certainly meet these guidelines, not all do.

Past donors need to be cultivated as potential prospects, and those who say "no" today may say "yes" tomorrow. Good stewardship is the key to future fundraising success.

- **Nurture your relationships with top prospects and donors.** This critical task requires the discipline to spend a significant amount of time off campus, including travel to other locations. Sometimes, prospects are not people you would normally befriend. Despite your differences, it is important to find ways of connecting.

- **Understand the organization and staffing of the development operation.** Provide development staff with prospect information you have gleaned and respond positively to suggestions for cultivation, solicitation, and stewardship activity.

- **Ensure that the chief development officer coordinates all staff and volunteer fundraising efforts.** The CDO should assign and oversee both cultivation and solicitation of prospects. Efficient organization is important so that staff members and volunteers are assigned appropriate prospects and the institution does not make embarrassing mistakes, such as soliciting the same donor twice for the same purpose.

- **Give credit publicly and often to everyone who participates in securing a gift.** Board members, administrators, faculty members, and volunteers all appreciate a president's public acknowledgment. Public praise validates individual effort as part of the fundraising team and encourages others to participate.

Chapter 5
Organizing for Fundraising

● ●

I am very aware that my final legitimacy or legacy will be very much determined by how successful we are in this campaign. That's just the hard fact of life.[11]

Walter Massey, Former President, Morehouse College

AN EFFECTIVE DEVELOPMENT OFFICE should be organized and staffed to conduct prospect research; provide stewardship of donors and prospects; conduct the annual fund, major gift, and planned giving programs; and, on occasion, conduct a campaign. An efficient, well-managed, and experienced development operation makes a president's fundraising responsibilities clear and more likely to be successful. By contrast, a disorganized development office undermines the efforts of a president. Even a president who is inexperienced in development will know when the operation is in trouble. The chief development officer must ensure a smooth-running development function that coordinates staff members, board

An efficient, well-managed, and experienced development operation makes a president's fundraising responsibilities clear and more likely to be successful. By contrast, a disorganized development office undermines the efforts of a president.

members, volunteers, and others, including the president, to meet fundraising goals. One of the basic keys for success is for major gifts officers and planned giving officers to spend most of their time on the road—the reason they are often called "road warriors."

In many higher education institutions, development is part of institutional advancement, which combines fundraising with the overlapping areas of alumni relations and public relations to create synergy and "advance" the institution's reputation and drawing power. The CDO is very likely the chief advancement officer and is often a vice president.

In some universities and colleges, alumni offices are independent of the institution in a structure that is deeply embedded in institutional culture and history. In such situations, the administration generally has little influence on alumni operations or materials. But separating alumni relations from development inhibits the full flowering of alumni philanthropy. Even when under the same umbrella, alumni professionals may insist that they are responsible for "friend raising" and not for fundraising when, in fact, friend raising and fundraising are inextricable.

When alumni are brought closer to the institution, their financial support increases. Alumni provide a vital source of support for the annual fund and capital projects. They are loyal to their alma mater as long as they perceive the institution to be supportive of them and respectful of their traditions. Alumni are also fickle about giving if they are distressed by an action by the president or board (for example, elimination of a sport, a radical change in the curriculum, or sanctions on a fraternity).

When I arrived at Rollins, I was impressed that the alumni board was raising money aggressively and saw fundraising as an integral part of its responsibilities. But not every successive board adopted that emphasis. Involvement very much reflected the board's composition and the alumni director's perspective. For the most part, our alumni directors did not think that they should be asking constituents for money. That attitude placed more responsibility for meeting annual fund goals on the annual fund staff.

While the alumni operation focused on involving and reconnecting alumni with the college, I participated by traveling around the country to meet key alumni and share our vision. We also developed stronger programs on campus to attract alumni to return for reunions and other events. Many alumni with whom I met said they had never had a visit from a president before; many said they had never been asked to contribute. Contrary to institutional lore, I found alumni to be very generous.

The public relations/communications office helps to increase the pride and connectedness of alumni, faculty members, students, parents, donors, and community leaders by reporting on institutional goals and achievements. At some institutions, communications is a stand-alone function reporting directly to the president. In others, it is part of the advancement office. Wherever located, regular communication to both internal and external constituencies connects people to the institution and creates an atmosphere of loyalty and support. Information and stories about

Alumni provide a vital source of support for the annual fund and capital projects. They are loyal to their alma mater as long as they perceive the institution to be supportive of them and respectful of their traditions.

the results of a campaign build understanding and enthusiasm. The advancement leader has the responsibility for helping these areas learn how they can support and promote each other.

Annual Fund: Learning to Give and Get

The annual fund instills the habit of giving. It is the bedrock of every development operation and a predictor of an institution's success in securing major gifts. This unrestricted and discretionary fund can give the president the flexibility to support institutional priorities. (At many institutions, however, the budget is balanced by the annual fund, and little or no discretion can be applied.)

A successful annual fund drive is a massive undertaking involving all development staff and many students, alumni, and others. The goal is to solicit as many constituents as possible and to increase the number and amount of contributions each year.

Many faculty and staff members support the annual fund, and some corporations are contributors. The most reliable and generous donors, though, are alumni and board members. Every board member should participate every year, and some institutions even have a minimum contribution for board members. Some exceptions may have to be made for those who do not have sufficient resources to contribute at the required level, but overall, a minimum-contribution requirement provides a guide for contributions and a stable amount of budgetary support each year.

The annual fund goal usually is negotiated by the president, chief financial officer, and chief development officer. Virtually all constituents are solicited—by phone, letter, or in person—and the funds are expended within a fiscal year. Some institutions engage outside consulting firms to conduct the fund drive. Mailings are part of the process, but person-to-person telephone solicitations, especially conducted by students and alumni, are most effective.

Traditionally, the president has a limited role in the annual fund. On occasion, however, the development staff at Rollins asked me to solicit an annual fund gift from a board member, major donor, or major prospect. I realized that certain prospects were worth the effort of a face-to-face annual fund solicitation. This interaction also prepared prospects for a major gift solicitation. In appropriate circumstances, a chief development officer will suggest that the president make a "double ask," coupling requests for an annual gift and a major gift.

At Rollins we also incorporated an appeal to parents into the annual fund drive. The board was concerned that parents might resent being asked for money while they were still paying tuition. But we pushed ahead with an aggressive parents' fund, with excellent results. Parents who had the resources and were satisfied with their children's progress were pleased to give. Many also made major gifts, especially during the campaign.

A caveat, however: Timing is important. The greatest parental fundraising successes occur during the student's second or third year, when parents are comfortable that all is going well, and they are not yet distracted by post-graduation issues. To assist the process, we established a parents' committee that focused primarily on fundraising but also provided feedback to the board and administration. This committee, chaired by an ex-officio member of the board, has been highly successful in engaging parents in the life of the college and encouraging lasting relationships among them.

Major Gifts: Short-Term and Long-Term Benefits

Major gifts represent a larger investment in programs, facilities, or other needs than do gifts to the annual fund. They can be unrestricted or restricted, current or planned, and they can take several years to secure. The president generally is involved in cultivating and soliciting major gift prospects.

From the president's perspective, each year there are unfunded projects and programs that would be of great benefit to the institution. A well-regarded young professor may have been requesting an expensive piece of equipment to enhance

When a prospect offers a much less significant gift than the one you have solicited, you can choose to accept it gracefully, or you can turn it down, expressing disappointment. My own philosophy is to accept the offer with thanks and keep the donor on the prospect list for another gift.

her research. Or a student lounge needs new furniture. Students and parents compare facilities among institutions and are attracted by up-to-date laboratories, residence halls, dining halls, gyms, and sports venues. Landscaping projects may also be desirable to improve an institution's curb appeal.

The development staff identifies prospects who might have the capacity and interest to make gifts in support of such initiatives. Institutions of different size and history consider different amounts of support (starting at $25,000 or $1 million) to be "major." Major gift funds are often expended within the year, although they may also be designated for the endowment or provided through a deferred instrument.

When a prospect offers a much less significant gift than the one you have solicited, you can choose to accept it gracefully, or you can turn it down, expressing disappointment. My own philosophy is to accept the offer with thanks and keep the donor on the prospect list for another gift. I confess, however, that on one fundraising trip, when the parent I was visiting offered me a gift far less than I had planned to request, I responded by saying that it was not sufficient and that I had hoped for more—and he did, in fact, increase his commitment. In such cases, it is important to understand whether the prospect was rejecting the project or the level of financial support requested.

There are also times when a prospect responds unpredictably. I visited with a parent from a well-known oil family in a large Texas city. He greeted me in his plush office, which boasted magnificent views all around. His response to my solicitation was that his family was not really connected to Rollins. Shocked, I said, "But your daughter is a student there." He responded by pointing out that no one in his family was sitting on our board or otherwise engaged in the institution. I found it difficult to believe that having a child in our residential undergraduate program did not qualify as family involvement.

Planned Giving

Major gifts include planned gifts, such as current gifts of personal property (for example, stock and real estate). Some people transfer a life-insurance policy, which can be cashed in or maintained. The biggest focus in planned giving is on bequests, annuities, trusts, and other instruments that commit a gift to the institution upon the donor's death and perhaps upon the death of the donor's spouse or other relatives. Because bequests are revocable, stewardship is vital so that these donors maintain a relationship with the institution.

Fundraising campaigns generally include a target for planned gifts, but presidents, board members, and development staff members are often less focused on such gifts because they do not satisfy current needs. It is shortsighted to neglect this aspect of philanthropy. Institutions that focus on planned giving ensure that they are building resources for the future, for while the institution may not benefit immediately, planned gifts provide for the needs of future students and faculty members. Most often, planned gifts provide much-needed additions to the endowment,

....

Institutions that focus on planned giving ensure that they are building resources for the future. While the institution may not benefit immediately, planned gifts provide for the needs of future students and faculty members.

which are otherwise difficult to secure. Further, many donors derive a great deal of satisfaction, as well as tax advantages, from making a planned gift.

The language in planned gift agreements should be as flexible as possible, since needs and priorities change over time. For example, an endowed chair in international business may have been funded by the time a bequest for that purpose matures. A donor interested in strengthening the business program might consider using more general language, such as a gift for a chair in business. Since the cost of an endowed chair might also change during the donor's lifetime, alternative language might call for establishing a scholarship endowment if a chair is not needed or if there are insufficient funds for a chair.

Presidents do not need to be experts in planned giving, but they should understand the general benefits and the circumstances that might encourage someone who cannot make an outright gift to be amenable to the idea of a trust or bequest instead. This area is a complicated one with numerous tax and legal ramifications, so access to a staff or volunteer expert is important.

Many board members are at the stage in life when they are developing their estate plans, which makes them good prospects for planned gifts in addition to outright gifts. They should periodically receive a review of the various planned giving vehicles and the benefits of planned gifts to the donor and to the institution.

Many institutions strengthen their ties to trust officers, lawyers, accountants, estate planners, and others who are critical to the planned giving program by bringing them to campus periodically for a thank-you luncheon. Planned giving societies, events, and publications are ways of thanking and maintaining ties with donors. They also inspire others to participate.

Mega Gifts: The Power to Transform

At the high end of major giving are mega gifts, which have the power to transform an institution. They are also called principal gifts, leadership gifts, legacy gifts, and ultimate gifts. There is tremendous satisfaction in securing a mega gift that sup-

There is no substitute for the president in developing the relationships, exploring the possibilities, and soliciting mega gifts. The president has to generate confidence in her or his leadership and make a compelling case for the transformative power of a mega gift—a process that can take years.

ports a much-needed project for the institution and provides a sense of pleasure and fulfillment to the donor. The potential for a mega gift is more likely in an individual's later years after a history of personal success and philanthropy.

A request that taps into a current wellspring of interest and philanthropy is most likely to succeed. Jerald Panas believes that "mega givers experience a spiritual sensation in their giving. . . . For many, when the major gift is made, there is a mystical soul-stirring which transcends the commonplace."[12] Whether prospects make gifts from a feeling of transcendence, a practical need, or a sense of compassion, each gift is special and helps to fulfill an institution's mission.

There is no substitute for the president in developing the relationships, exploring the possibilities, and soliciting mega gifts. The president has to generate confidence in her or his leadership and make a compelling case for the transformative power of a mega gift—a process that can take years. Likely prospects for such gifts have great financial capacity, are close to the institution (often serving on the board), and are familiar with its vision, strategic plans, needs, and potential.

In the 1980s, the Woodruff brothers gave Emory University $105 million in Coca-Cola stock, enabling the university to reposition itself as one of America's top universities. Emory's leadership invested the gift in the recruitment of top faculty members and students, construction of state-of-the-art facilities, and extending the institution's reputation. In 2005, Rollins received a bequest of more than

$100 million, with few restrictions as to its use. The gift was the result of the work of three presidents, numerous development staff members, administrators, board members, and faculty members who befriended and spent time with the donor.

Whenever an institution receives a mega gift, development leaders worry about their ability to continue and grow constituent giving. The size of both gifts raised concerns that others might not continue to support the university or would consider their gifts too small and inconsequential to make a difference. But at both Emory and Rollins, giving has increased, not declined. No matter the size of the institution's budget, a nine-figure gift can be transformative if carefully applied and responsibly managed.

In recent years there has been an upsurge in mega gifts, even during recessionary periods. The estimated $41 trillion transfer of wealth from baby boomers to their children and grandchildren continues to be a boon for higher education. Paul G. Schervish and John J. Havens, professors at Boston College, predicted the magnitude of this intergenerational transfer of wealth in 1999 and have reaffirmed the amount several times since then.[13] Many affluent families include their children in giving decisions to prepare them for the responsibilities of philanthropy.

Warren Buffett, along with Bill and Melinda Gates, issued a challenge in 2010, the Giving Pledge, calling on billionaires to give half of their wealth to charity. This initiative is important because even the super-rich are influenced by their peers to live in certain communities, shop in certain stores, attend certain schools, engage in certain activities, and give to certain charities. A mega gift made by a friend or acquaintance often triggers other significant gifts from those eager to establish their status and contribute to causes in which they believe.

- **Identify the building blocks of an efficient and effective development operation** and ensure that the structure and staffing are appropriate for your institution and its needs. Assign a competent chief development officer or advancement vice president the challenge of assembling, organizing, and assessing a highly motivated and productive staff and coordinating all efforts to meet fundraising goals.

- **Insist on synergy among advancement programs and activities.** Especially when development is combined with alumni relations and public relations, these offices must communicate well and coordinate their efforts.

- **Focus your own fundraising on major and mega gifts.** Prospects at this level generally expect and respond to personal interaction with the president. Be certain, however, that the annual fund and planned giving programs are successful and that revenue is increasing annually.

- **If the development operation is unable to produce the results that you and the board expect, bring in a consultant or an experienced development officer** to assess the operation and staff and make recommendations. If a major overhaul is required, begin with an assessment of the chief development officer and consider other major changes. If changes are necessary, do not procrastinate.

Chapter 6
Asking for Money

• •

To solicit funds is not to go, cap in hand, begging
support for some marginal activity. It is, instead,
to invite a friend to share in the privilege of
the greatest partnership of all—the quest for
knowledge, on which our present existence and
our future well-being depend.[14]

Frank H.T. Rhodes, President Emeritus, Cornell University

EVEN WITH A STRONG DEVELOPMENT BACKGROUND, during my
first few years at Rollins I frequently worried that I would not live up to the expectations my constituents had of me. What if I could not raise money in this new
environment? What if I was not accepted? What if I did not radiate confidence and
articulate a compelling vision?

The bottom line to fundraising success is asking, asking, asking. Presidents who
are successful solicitors are not embarrassed to be asking. They readily reveal their
passion for the institution they lead and for the projects they are proposing.

Soliciting a gift is not begging. Rather, it gives a prospect the opportunity to
participate in a great enterprise that teaches students to become good citizens,
solves social and medical problems, and contributes to economic development.

But people need to have a relationship with the institution or develop one before they consider a gift. If we do not cultivate and solicit them, they will give elsewhere. People are often moved to give if they have great confidence in the president and believe in his or her vision and goals. The president is the living embodiment of the institution's accomplishments and aspirations, with great personal authority and influence. Fundraisers believe in the simple adage that people give to people. Prospects are honored and flattered to be solicited by the president, and solicitations made by presidents generally yield more generous gifts than solicitations by others. Some have never before been solicited and are first-time donors. Once they have made a gift, these donors expect to have regular contact with the president.

Why People Give

Philosophers, sociologists, and other scholars have proposed numerous explanations and interpretations for giving. One of the first was Maimonides, the 12th-century rabbi, philosopher, and physician, who proposed eight different levels of *tzedakah* (charity). He considered the two highest levels to be anonymous giving and the provision of support to help a person in need become independent, and the two lowest to be giving cheerfully but less than one should, and giving grudgingly.

Understanding how people view personal philanthropy and what motivates them to give can help prepare us for successful solicitations. I have known people with vast resources who were generous and altruistic, giving funds to a variety of organizations where they might make a real difference. Their charitable giving brings them a great deal of personal satisfaction. Others give because they are

Prospects are honored and flattered to be solicited by the president, and solicitations made by presidents generally yield more generous gifts than solicitations by others.

When we know something about a donor's motivations, we can craft a strategy and a request that appeal to a prospect's best impulses, guilt, sense of obligation, or competitiveness with a peer.

moved by the plight of a child or an overlooked community need.

Most donors I have known, however, expect to engage in a reciprocal transaction: a gift to satisfy an institution's need in return for personal recognition, contact with the president, a board seat, or some other benefit. When we know something about a donor's motivations, we can craft a strategy and a request that appeal to a prospect's best impulses, guilt, sense of obligation, or competitiveness with a peer. As Hank Rosso, founding director of the Fund Raising School at Indiana University's Center for Philanthropy, famously said, "fundraising is the gentle art of teaching people the joy of giving."[15]

I like to group motivations for giving into three categories: spiritual, pragmatic, and emotional. It is important to recognize that motivations may overlap or change over time. A thoughtful solicitor will seek to understand and appeal to a prospect's *current* motivation for giving. For this reason, a president should be well prepared with background on an individual and attuned to the nuances of his or her reactions. A president should talk with others who are close to the prospect, study the prospect's background and interests, and listen carefully to his or her comments. Board members can often provide useful insights about people they know. Another good way of gaining insight into motivations is to ask previous donors why they contributed.

Spiritual Philanthropy

People who are spiritually motivated give to their religious organizations and to faith-based colleges or universities. These donors may also be inspired to support opportunities in secular institutions, such as religious studies or service experiences for students. One donor was so impressed by the change in student attitudes after a service experience in a small town in a South American country that she established an endowment to ensure that any student interested in the program would have at least some financial support. This donor spent time with students before they left for their program and even more time when they returned. She suggested that returning students speak to their peers about their experiences and how their values changed as a result of the program. Clearly, the donor was as excited about the program as the students were.

Spiritual giving may also stem from a sense that a project or program has the potential to solve an intractable social problem and improve society. For spiritually motivated donors, supporting such a project is uplifting and noble. They may feel called to use their resources to improve society and provide a helping hand to those less fortunate.

Pragmatic Philanthropy

Pragmatic philanthropy is stimulated by a desire to enhance one's business, social mobility, reputation, or status. Pragmatic philanthropy also brings donors into a network of people with whom they wish to interact. These motivators for giving are common, and there is nothing inappropriate about them. Colleges and universities are well positioned to fulfill these needs through membership in volunteer groups and participation in donor-recognition events. Although donors may say that they do not care about recognition, many of them do, but they may be too modest or embarrassed to be assertive about it. Presidents and development officers must handle this issue with great sensitivity.

Business leaders especially are accustomed to a kind of reciprocity in soliciting gifts for their favorite charities. With such donors it helps to mention peers who have contributed. They may also be motivated by the tax benefits of giving. Finally, many donors give because of peer pressure or peer example. Once the habit takes hold, they derive great pleasure in being among the generous leaders in the community.

Some successful entrepreneurs want to combine their business acumen with their dollars to solve a challenging educational or social problem. Venture philanthropy, sometimes called social entrepreneurship, has benefits for both donor and institution. But a donor partnership should be consistent with the mission and goals of the institution and be designed carefully with tax laws regarding charitable donations in mind. This type of philanthropy is grantmaking based on principles that venture capitalists use when investing in new businesses. After identifying a problem, the entrepreneur applies his or her knowledge, experience, and funds toward the search for a solution. Such donors are prepared to make a long-term investment but insist on clear goals, operational plans, and accountability measures. They often become personally involved on the board or management team of the project.

Emotional Philanthropy

Emotional giving tends to be derived from experience or heartfelt sympathy with a cause or a person who exemplifies that cause. Examples abound: Those who went through college on a scholarship often are motivated to provide the same benefit to others. Some are drawn to philanthropy for medical research to find solutions and cures for diseases that may afflict them or their families. For others, enthusiasm for a competitive athletic team can drive philanthropic interest.

When attracting such emotional support, we must be careful not to manipulate the feelings of prospects. Handled with sensitivity, there is nothing wrong with raising money for an appropriate memorial project soon after the death of a beloved family member or friend. Emotions are strong at this moment, and others will be moved to contribute as well.

Donors may be interested solely in the programs with which they have special connections while their ties to the institution as a whole may be weak. But these relationships have limits. Increasingly, we are learning that diverse groups must be treated differently in fundraising. For example, development professionals are creating tailored approaches for women and minority groups rather than applying traditional fundraising techniques across the board.

My experience suggests that women's giving interests often revolve around opportunities for college-age and returning women students. Women's philanthropy is less tied to their spouses' interests than it used to be— especially among working women who want to improve opportunities for the next generation of girls and women. Giving by organized women's groups has increased at a faster rate than giving by the overall foundation community. A number of organizations— such as the Women's Philanthropy Institute at the Indiana University Center on Philanthropy—offer research, education, and information on women and philanthropy.

In the past, many colleges and universities failed to engage African Americans and Hispanics in their fundraising activities. We are just learning that some minority communities give a larger proportion of their discretionary funds than others. This habit developed as a result of government and business inaction on programs and projects of interest to these communities. According to Chacona Johnson, affiliated with the University of Michigan and the Detroit Public Schools Foundation, African-American giving has been, and still is, based in churches. She adds that until recently many major institutions did not fully engage with the black community.[16] It is time to enlist all of our constituents in providing philanthropic support for our institutions. One way to achieve this goal is to segment our populations and involve them appropriately. The effort has already begun.

Motivation and Solicitation: What Works and What Doesn't

When soliciting gifts from major donors, presidents need to keep the donor's giving history and motivation in mind. People need to be involved, cultivated, and solicited. Consider these two presidential approaches:

1. The president invites a major donor to the university for lunch and solicits her for a lead gift for the planned sports center. This long-time donor has a history of making significant lead gifts for transformational academic projects and programs. She seems lukewarm toward the sports-center project, but it is a high priority for the president, who urges her to support it and names people in the donor's circle who have contributed. Although the prospect is not showing enthusiasm, the president presses on, hoping to secure a gift. By the time the lunch meeting ends, both parties are uncomfortable, and nothing has been resolved. In fact, the president may have lost a potentially large campaign gift by failing to connect with this donor's giving interests.

2. The college is gearing up for a blockbuster of a campaign, with a goal four times larger than the amount raised in its previous campaign. The board is nervous, and so is the staff. One long-time staff member tells the president that while alumni love the college, they do not give money. Accepting this challenge, the president focuses on alumni of means, whether or not they have ever supported the college. She and the development staff make numerous cultivation visits and work hard at on-campus alumni events. Whenever possible, the president talks about the institution's history, values, and ambitions. Alumni around the country are excited and interested. More of them return each year for reunions as the college improves the experience. And the president and others begin to sit down and talk with individual alumni about the need for their support. The campaign concludes triumphantly, exceeding its financial target. Alumni provided many significant gifts for the endowment and facilities. The president learned that alumni had not been contributing because they had not been involved or solicited.

The second example is my story at Rollins. I was thrilled at the end of the campaign to be able to report the extraordinary contributions of alumni to the future of the institution they love. When we published the numbers, I was proud to report that alumni had funded more than half the campaign.

Prepping the President

The more solicitations presidents make, the more money they raise. To be successful, presidents should set aside time for frequent, planned, one-on-one cultivation and solicitation activities, in addition to the time spent interacting briefly with many prospects and donors at special events. It is up to the development office to help the president understand the timing and setting for a solicitation. If the president has a short list of important solicitations and appropriate targets, she or he can make the request anywhere, from the theater to the basketball arena. Of course, this approach is less desirable than a planned opportunity to sit down together, but it can work.

Certain fundamental materials and arrangements will smooth the way for solicitation meetings:

- *Participants.* Decide whether anyone should join the president in the solicitation and whether someone (for example, a spouse or an advisor) should be invited to accompany the prospect. I found that too often we asked a male prospect to a solicitation meeting without his spouse. Many couples make philanthropic decisions together, so this issue must be addressed carefully. In setting up the appointment, ask the prospect whether his or her spouse should participate.

- *Briefing memorandum.* The president and others involved in the meeting

The more solicitations presidents make, the more money they raise. To be successful, presidents should set aside time for frequent, planned, one-on-one cultivation and solicitation activities.

need a thorough briefing memorandum that includes background on the prospect, information about the project being proposed, and the amount being requested. My colleagues and I have made serious blunders without an accurate and comprehensive review of a prospect's background and interests, especially an alumnus' experiences at the institution and relationship to his classmates.

- *Contact.* If the planned solicitation is of a board member or major prospect, the president or a board member should make the telephone call to set up the appointment and explain why the meeting is requested. This way, the prospect feels respected and knows what the meeting is about. Acceptance of the appointment is a good sign. If the prospect's assistant insists on making the appointment, be sure that the person making the call is thoughtful and respectful.

- *Meeting location.* The atmosphere of a restaurant, home, or office makes a difference to the pacing and style of the solicitation. Many presidents have horror stories to tell about the noisy restaurant where they tried unsuccessfully to solicit a major gift or the uncomfortable moment when it was unclear who would pick up the check.

Even experienced presidents should rehearse an important solicitation with the chief development officer and/or the volunteer who is participating. Too often, a meeting goes extremely well and everyone enjoys the conversation, but no one actually solicits the prospect. The president should debrief with the chief development officer so that information about the process and the prospect goes into the file. This kind of information is extraordinarily valuable for the development staff as relationships between institutional representatives and prospects are cultivated.

The payoff for the president's investment of time and effort in the cultivation and successful solicitation of prospects is threefold:

- Giving donors the pleasure of making transformational gifts;

- Securing support for needed facilities, faculty chairs, student scholarships, and programs; and

- Generating enthusiasm for the results among the faculty members, students, and alumni.

Suggestions for Making the Solicitation

After all the work of identifying and cultivating promising prospects and then preparing to meet with them, it's time to solicit the gift. I call the process of solicitation "Ask with CCLASS."

1. *Chat:* Get comfortable with the prospect. Create a relaxed atmosphere by chatting about such things as families, vacations, and the business environment.

2. *Case:* Review briefly your institution's achievements and goals. Make the case for the project for which you are seeking funding. Communicate the project's importance, its transformational potential, and your passion for it.

3. *Listen:* As you weave the story of the impact this project will have on the institution, listen carefully to the prospect's responses and watch for non-verbal reactions as well. If the prospect is engaged and listening carefully, you can assume you are on the right track. It often helps to mention others who have supported the project. If the prospect seems lukewarm to the project, explore other options that are also important to the institution's mission.

4. *Ask:* When you have made your case and responded to the prospect's questions, ask for the gift. Be specific about the dollar amount, and make no apologies.

5. *Stop talking:* Once you have made the solicitation, be quiet. It takes a prospect time to process the request and the magnitude of the support requested. This is the hardest part of the transaction; it is similar to a teacher asking

the class a question and being greeted with silence. Instead of continuing to talk, an experienced teacher knows to wait quietly. People will respond.

6. *Show me the money:* Do not leave the meeting without an agreement about follow-up. If the prospect agrees to the request, discuss a payment schedule. Some donors fulfill the entire pledge within a short period, but many pay over five years or more. Ask whether you may send over a pledge form in the next few days. (Optimistic presidents often carry the forms in their pockets.) The prospect may wish to confer with a lawyer, trust officer, spouse, or other party. It is not unusual for a prospect to want some time to think about the proposal or to ask for something in writing. In such circumstances, establish a time when you can call to follow up.

If the prospect declines to participate, the president needs to ascertain whether the project is not appealing or the amount requested is inappropriate at this time due to other commitments. If the prospect explains why, the president should respond with questions about appropriate follow-up. A good question is, "When may I come back to you with another proposal?" Often, a significant gift takes a number of visits and conversations. It is important not to be impatient and to remember that you are asking a lot. A decline is not a personal rejection. Always thank the prospect for taking the time to discuss the institution with you, and send a follow-up note afterward.

Presidents who rehearse a solicitation do better than those who do not; presidents who make more solicitations are more successful than those who make fewer. With time and practice, the successes will mount and confidence will grow. A president's confidence inspires prospects to get involved and provide support. It is a cycle worth pursuing.

Opportunity Fundraising

The typical fundraising process—identifying, cultivating, and soliciting the prospect—takes time and yields results. In fact, experienced fundraisers suggest between 5 and 10 cultivation practices, or "moves," before the solicitation. From time to time, however, an opportunity arises that the president can seize. Given the right circumstances, the president should ignore the usual stages and make an unplanned and unscheduled solicitation.

Here are some examples of auspicious moments for impromptu solicitations:

- You have traveled across the country and are having dinner with a highly successful and prominent alumnus. Although this is the first time you have met him, he appears to be engaged, interested, and absorbed in your description of the institutional vision, strategic plan, and campaign opportunities. Why not ask if he would consider a gift toward a project that you believe would be of interest?

- At a party in the university museum, you are talking with a prospect who asks you how the campaign is going. Why not ask if she will consider becoming part of an effort to expand the museum?

- A couple bicycling across campus on a Saturday morning stops to talk to you. They are highly complimentary about the beauty of the campus. Why not ask if they would contribute to the completion of the lakefront landscaping?

> **Presidents who rehearse a solicitation do better than those who do not; presidents who make more solicitations are more successful than those who make fewer. With time and practice, the successes will mount and confidence will grow.**

- You are on the phone with a parent prospect whom you rarely see or talk with. He is very satisfied with his son's education and his interest in continuing on for a master's degree in business. Why not solicit this parent for an endowed chair in business?

Each of these examples is a true story, and each resulted in a gift. Such impromptu requests shortcut the cultivation cycle, but if it feels right, do it. Such casual and spontaneous interactions would not usually be identified as opportunities, but presidents can take advantage of a warm exchange to ask for philanthropic support. Presidents should trust their instincts in such situations and not be constrained by the customary process for working with prospects.

- **Contribute generously to the annual fund, and make a personal gift to a campaign.** The president is an example to others; other administrators should also be encouraged to participate. Personal giving makes it easier and more appropriate to ask others to contribute. It is also a matter of pride.

- **Prepare thoroughly for every solicitation.** As you craft your request, try to understand your prospect's giving interests and motivations. Study his or her history, connections with the institution, financial situation, and prior giving. Be familiar with the purpose, need, and cost of the proposed project. A good research office should provide those materials for you.

- **Practice for a solicitation.** A president's essential steps are to establish a rapport with the prospect, be specific about the purpose and amount of the request, be silent after the solicitation is made, and establish follow-up steps. You can never rehearse too much. To become comfortable, try a role-playing activity. Involve any volunteer, faculty member, or staff member who will accompany you. Debrief with the chief development officer after every solicitation so that you can plan the follow up and ensure that the information you secure—both factual and anecdotal— is recorded.

- **Engage in opportunity fundraising when appropriate.** Despite the customary formulas for cultivation and solicitation of prospects, there are times to seize the moment. Learn to trust your own instincts about what approach to follow with a particular individual and when it is advisable to change course.

Chapter 7
Campaigning for Change

● ●

When I became chancellor of UCLA in 1968, I did not imagine that I would one day lead a $300-million capital campaign to be followed eight years later by one for more than $1 billion. . . . We have had to adjust to an era of constrained resources and increased competition for every dollar.[17]

Charles E. Young, Chancellor Emeritus, University of California, Los Angeles

AS A VEHICLE FOR ORGANIZING the fundraising program, a campaign imposes discipline on fundraisers and focuses the philanthropy of constituents by creating a sense of common purpose. A campaign generates excitement and provides many opportunities to tell the institution's story and to enlist all stakeholders in the endeavor. A successful campaign also provides flexible financial resources that the president and board can use as an incentive to promote needed change. A *capital campaign* seeks funding for facilities and endowment, while a *comprehensive campaign* includes expendable gifts for the annual fund and special projects, in-kind gifts, and capital and planned gifts.

A campaign focuses everyone on the institution's goals and needs. It must be grounded in the vision, mission, and strategic direction of the institution. A well-crafted, well-conducted, and well-publicized campaign is an opportunity to improve and transform the institution. When it is well executed, a campaign not only attracts significant resources, but enhances the institution's quality and reputation.

These days, universities and colleges are in an almost perpetual campaign mode. The needs are so great and the traditional funding sources so unpredictable that institutions must increasingly focus on philanthropy. A typical campaign has a quiet phase of about three years to raise the largest gifts and set the goal, followed by a public phase of five years. Campaign fundraising is typically handled sequentially, starting with prospects for the largest gifts. Experience has shown that this approach raises the most money, which means that pressure to run what used to be called "the every man a dollar campaign" should be resisted. Almost as soon as one campaign is concluded, the quiet phase of the next one begins. If too much time elapses between campaigns, the focus and discipline of the development staff, board members, and volunteers relaxes, and connections with prospects and donors weaken. It becomes difficult to gear up again.

An effective campaign grows organically from the institutional culture, featuring a powerful case for support based on the strategic plan and a list of gift opportunities and their pricing. The case statement is a brief, focused rationale for the campaign drafted or at least approved by the president. What does the institution wish to accomplish that will excite donors, and how do those goals relate to the strategic plan? Once the case has been developed, no campaign should be launched without:

- Active presidential leadership;

These days, universities and colleges are in an almost perpetual campaign mode. The needs are so great and the traditional funding sources so unpredictable that institutions must increasingly focus on philanthropy.

- A committed board and other volunteers who serve on various campaign committees;
- A highly qualified development staff; and
- A deep pool of prospects.

If, however, all of those elements are not in place, but the president and board still insist on moving forward with a campaign, the process can serve as an organizing mechanism to strengthen the institution's capacity for fundraising.

Presidents who come from the academic side of higher education may have had limited involvement in institutional fundraising campaigns. In their presidential role, they must become active cheerleaders and fundraisers for periodic campaigns. At the University of Miami in the 1980s, for example, the president insisted on a much more ambitious campaign goal than the board was prepared to set, and the compromise was a number far greater than our consultants had recommended. I learned that new presidents have a lot of capital that they can spend on issues important to them. The audacity of the goal propelled us to success, and we exceeded it.

The president charted a bold and exciting vision for the university, and we had a strong board, active volunteer groups, a significant number of prospects, and a good development staff. Another key to our success was the visibility and influence of our campaign chair, who was also the board chair and a legend in the community. He was unafraid to solicit mega gifts from anyone with resources. He made his own generous gift at the beginning of the campaign and often said, "After I bellied up to the bar, I could ask anyone for anything." Retired, he also gave the campaign a lot of his time. In response to the excitement and leadership of the campaign, we were also able to enlist vice presidents, deans, volunteers, and board members in soliciting funds for a campaign that ultimately elevated the university's national status.

At Rollins in the 1990s, too, an ambitious campaign was necessary. The need and potential were so great that I did not doubt that the campaign would be successful. We transformed the college with a large number of endowed chairs and much-needed facilities. We purchased properties to expand our small campus, and we developed several revenue-producing commercial projects despite the reservations of some board members. I was fortunate to have board chairs who were not afraid to support our initiatives and take some risks.

Although I had some anxiety about my ability to raise money in a new environment, I just kept at it. A few prospects crossed the street when they saw me coming; others gave less than they could have.

Fortunately, though, there were enough donors to help us raise more than $160 million—$60 million over the goal. I found that there is no substitute for telling the story and asking everyone to join in the effort to transform the institution. By the end of the campaign, we had significantly improved the college's financial health and academic quality, as well as its reputation. Several factors contributed to our fundraising success: a great story to tell, a large number of wealthy alumni and parents who had never been solicited systematically, a series of excellent campaign chairs from the board, a productive staff, and many solicitations.

Still, we did hit some rough patches on the road to completion. About two-thirds of the way into the campaign, the chief development officer came into my office and announced that we were out of prospects and would have to terminate the campaign early. We solved the problem by agreeing to go back to our earliest and most generous donors. And, indeed, many of them made additional gifts. At a board executive-committee meeting, when I gave my president's report, I men-

---

Several factors contributed to our fundraising success at Rollins: a great story to tell, a large number of wealthy alumni and parents who had never been solicited systematically, a series of excellent campaign chairs from the board, a productive staff, and many solicitations.

The president's first step is to invite the academic leadership—deans and vice presidents—to work with faculty and staff in developing a list of needs that grow out of the mission and strategic plan. With this solid grounding, the campaign will be seen as supporting institutional goals.

tioned that we needed $750,000 more to begin construction on a new concert hall. A board member who had already given to that project asked when we would begin construction if we had all the funding. I said that as soon as we had a signed commitment for the remainder we would put the shovel in the ground. He pledged the money, and because of his advanced age I sent the CDO back to the office to get a pledge form. We started construction almost immediately.

Identifying Needs and Priorities

When launching a campaign, the president's first step is to invite the academic leadership—deans and vice presidents—to work with faculty and staff in developing a list of needs that grow out of the mission and strategic plan. With this solid grounding, the campaign will be seen as supporting institutional goals. This process also gives faculty members a meaningful role in the campaign.

Next, the president reviews and revises the draft list with the chief academic officer and the chief development officer. Since more needs are always identified than can be fulfilled in a single campaign, the list must then be pruned and prioritized. Each identified need should be accompanied by the level of support required from philanthropy.

The final list will not satisfy everyone. Faculty members will importune the president and academic vice president to reinstate items they consider vital to their departments and their work. Administrators may find other ways of securing some of the identified needs that do not make it to the list. It helps if there is something for every department on the final needs list.

When the list is ready, the president brings it to the board for discussion and formal approval. To ensure involvement at all levels, the list of needs and pricing should also be accepted as feasible by the development committee (at an independent institution) or the foundation board (at a public institution), since they will have a major responsibility for fulfilling the campaign goals.

Early in the process, a consultant may be engaged to conduct a feasibility study to assess the case for support, determine the readiness of prospects to contribute, and estimate how much money can be raised. Such a study involves confidential in-person interviews with major and potential donors. A feasibility study is not absolutely necessary, but it is a good tool to help determine if an institution is ready to launch a campaign. It is helpful to secure a gift to fund the study.

Funding the Campaign

Managing a successful campaign requires adequate resources. Such investments should begin several years before the campaign start date. Opinions vary on how much a campaign should cost, but institutions generally spend about 10 to 15 percent of the campaign goal, depending on the size and scope of the campaign and the ongoing level of support and staffing. Campaign budgets include additional costs for events, entertainment, travel, counsel, databases and technology, publications, and staff.

Covering the increased costs of a campaign is challenging, so the president, chief development officer, and chief financial officer need to spend time reviewing the funding options in light of the institution's financial picture. Then the president makes a recommendation to the board, which considers the sources and purposes of the campaign budget and ultimately puts its stamp of approval on all elements of the campaign. Campaign costs can be covered through a tax on all participating university units; built into the annual budget; drawn from the endowment, unrestricted funds, or bequests; or taken as a percentage of each gift. If a percentage of each gift is applied, donors should be made aware of this policy. In a public institution, the related foundation may also be a source of campaign funding.

A note: It is generally a mistake to reduce the development staff after a campaign. A significant reduction undermines the staff's ability to perform at newly established levels. One of the main functions of a campaign is to raise the institution's capacity to achieve permanently higher giving levels.

Finding the Right Volunteer Leader

A crucial step in campaign preparation is enlisting the right person to chair the campaign. This choice can mean the difference between success and failure. While the role is a great honor, it is also demanding: The chair needs the time, influence, and visibility to bring the institution's message to external groups; a sound understanding of the institution and the campaign; and the ability to open doors for the president, vice president, and key volunteers. It is vital that the chair make an early and generous financial commitment to the campaign. During the campaign, the chair should refrain from raising money for other organizations. He or she should also identify volunteers for other leadership positions and campaign committees.

A key element in the choice of a campaign chair is the person's relationship with the president. They should form a mutually supportive team that also works well with the chief development officer. On occasion, the campaign chair is also the board chair.

At Rollins, I consulted closely with the board leadership to identify successive chairs for the campaign. I always made it clear that a campaign chair is obligated

A crucial step in campaign preparation is enlisting the right person to chair the campaign. This choice can mean the difference between success and failure.

to set an example by making a significant gift, and each chair did so. It was exhilarating to watch these individuals become increasingly comfortable with soliciting big gifts.

Creating Campaign Policies

When a campaign is launched at an independent college or university, the development committee and the full board review and accept the case statement, the list of needs and pricing, and the campaign structure, timing, and financial target. At a public institution, the foundation and institutional boards collaborate to approve these measures. The president and chief development officer work with the board to clarify and codify decisions on fundraising and campaigns in a series of policies.

One key policy decision is what to include in campaign reports—for example, whether and how to include bequests. The Council for Advancement and Support of Education (CASE) has developed standards for campaign reporting and compiles and disseminates comparative campaign data annually.[18] Institutions must be scrupulous in providing accurate data for this report.

Board campaign policies generally address:

- How the campaign will be funded;
- How to count and report pledges, real property, insurance, bequests, and trusts;
- Whether planned gifts are part of the campaign;
- The basis for naming projects, programs, and buildings for donors;
- Whether capital projects may be started before funding is completely committed;
- Whether to build a maintenance endowment into the pricing of construction projects; and
- Whether undesignated current gifts and bequests are considered budget relieving or budget additive.

Even experienced leaders often turn to consultants to guide them in the complex details of running a campaign. An outside consultant can be objective, keep everyone focused on campaign preparation and implementation, and help to professionalize the development operation.

Using a Consultant

If the president, board, chief development officer, and development staff are not sufficiently experienced, it may be wise to engage a fundraising consultant. Even experienced leaders often turn to consultants to guide them in the complex details of running a campaign. An outside consultant can be objective, keep everyone focused on campaign preparation and implementation, and help to professionalize the development operation. In many cases, the consultant provides the margin of difference between modest and unprecedented fundraising success. Consultants can operate on-site (the most expensive option) or can visit periodically, especially for meetings of the advancement staff, senior administrators, and boards. They can assist in training the staff members and the volunteers and serve as a personal fundraising advisor to the CDO, campaign chair, and president. A successful campaign easily covers the expense of one or more consultants. The president, board chair, campaign chair, and chief development officer should all be involved in the selection because the consultant becomes part of their executive team for the campaign.

Setting the Goal

Once the president and chief development officer are satisfied with the quality of the prospect pool, the list of funding opportunities, the strength of the development staff, and the leadership of the board, they should propose a tentative fundraising goal for the campaign. During this "quiet phase" of a campaign, which lasts two or three years, the institution determines whether the goal is appropriate based on the amount of money committed by board members and top prospects. Board commitments should represent roughly 30 to 40 percent of the goal. Beyond that, any goal depends, in large part, on the potential in the institution's prospect pool. A gift-range table based on a tentative goal helps to clarify how many gifts of what size will be needed. Nationally, a greater and greater percentage of campaign funds is generated from fewer and fewer donors. About 90 percent or more of the goal comes from 10 to 20 percent of donors or less. Such numbers make it clear that top donors deserve a great deal of personal attention from the president and the board. Experience shows that three or four prospects are solicited for every one that agrees to make a gift. If the pool lacks sufficient depth and ability, the president might put the brakes on a campaign until there is time to cultivate more prospects.

A campaign goal should be ambitious but not foolish. Frequently, boards, development staff, and presidents are cautious about setting a big target because they want to be successful. Fundraising consultants also want to ensure success and often recommend a goal they know is feasible. But a challenging goal with a compelling case for support and a transformational list of opportunities has the power to excite constituents. Some modest donors may feel that their contributions will not make a difference toward a large goal, but many people are inspired by a higher goal that has the potential to effect real change. I learned from the University of Miami president to be bold when setting a goal. I did the same thing at Rollins. In both cases, these campaigns put us in the big leagues.

When the campaign begins to attract significant gifts, others want to be part of

....

A challenging goal with a compelling case for support and a transformational list of opportunities has the power to excite constituents.

the effort, and this growing enthusiasm can cause a snowball effect. People like to be on a winning team. When all the right elements are in place, the campaign can be launched publicly with significant fanfare. At donor-oriented events, the president and board chair can thank publicly those who have been generous and encourage others to participate. (Even if donors deny it, I have found that most are pleased to be recognized in front of their peers.) Depending on the progress of fundraising, as the campaign nears its conclusion, the president needs to recommend to the board whether to raise the goal, extend the campaign time frame, or exceed the goal. The public phase generally lasts five years and is followed by a victory celebration honoring donors.

There is little difference between the goal-setting and fundraising approaches of public and independent institutions. The elements of success are the same. As the percentage of institutional budgets that states provide has diminished over the years, public institutions and systems have increased their development staffs, mounted aggressive fundraising operations, and achieved huge campaign goals. In a *Chronicle of Higher Education* update on fundraising campaigns with goals of $1 billion and more, 20 of the 36 institutions reporting were public. Although the top five were independent, the next eight were public institutions.[19]

Typical Concerns

A campaign is a challenging undertaking that generates long periods of optimism and high energy, but also moments when the board and staff are concerned that things are not progressing as well as they could. Periodically, the president, the board, and even the CDO and development staff may question whether the goal is attainable and become anxious about the possibility of failure. The following concerns will sound familiar to anyone who has been involved in a campaign.

- **"We cannot reach our goal."** Near the end of a campaign, staff and board members begin to fret that they will not achieve the fundraising goal. The remaining prospect list looks thin, and the goal seems out of reach. Despite her or his private worries, the president needs to exude complete confidence and optimism and encourage discipline and good development work. Remind the team that it is good practice to go back to early donors since they often are willing to make additional commitments.

- **"Everyone has fundraising fatigue."** It is natural for energy and enthusiasm to reach a low point during a campaign. This is the time for the president to rally the troops by giving an encouraging and uplifting talk about the need for and likelihood of success. People need to be reminded about the transformational potential of the campaign: The resources garnered serve as an investment in the students of today and tomorrow. Above all, the president must remain personally optimistic and enthusiastic. Celebrate the victories achieved thus far and the prospect of success just across the horizon.

- **"We are five years into a campaign, so why aren't our salaries more competitive?"** Although the president may have warned people during the planning phase that a campaign does not usually satisfy certain continuing needs, they probably have forgotten those words. Among those needs are faculty salaries and facility maintenance. The president's role is to focus on the successes and work to strengthen the budget to deal with ongoing financial problems.

TIPS FOR PRESIDENTS

- **The quiet phase of a campaign is a test of how much the institution can raise.** Use this time aggressively to practice your cultivation and solicitation skills as you pursue the large gifts that are generated before the public campaign launch. During this phase, test a campaign goal that is ambitious but attainable. Such a goal focuses everyone's attention on the management of prospects, cultivation and stewardship activities, and the need for a significant number of solicitations.

- **Be sure that you are consulted on the selection of a campaign chair.** The president, campaign chair, and chief development officer are the top team and must work well together.

- **Promote a positive role in the campaign for faculty and staff.** Setting fundraising priorities requires communication and collaboration, guided by the president and other administrators. Not all needs can be met in a campaign, but a genuinely participatory process makes compromise easier.

- **Project confidence and enthusiasm throughout the campaign.** You are the pivot around which the campaign operates, and everyone else's morale depends on yours— especially when a campaign hits the inevitable bumps in the road.

Chapter 8

Accepting, Declining, and Managing Gifts

Since the faculty was almost fully tenured,
I could change Smith's culture only by raising
new resources.[20]

Jill Ker Conway, President Emerita, Smith College

SOME PRESIDENTS ARE SO HUNGRY for fundraising success that they will accept virtually any proffered gift. If they do, their action may, unfortunately, be costly for the institution.

Presidents and boards should exercise discretion about the gifts they accept. Some are not worth taking.

Presidents and boards should exercise discretion about the gifts they accept. Some are not worth taking. These decisions will differ among institutions depending on financial conditions and needs, so it is important to have policies in place that will provide guidance on gift acceptance. The development staff should take the lead in drafting appropriate policies, and the development committee of the board or foundation board should review and approve them.

Assessing the Value and Cost of Gifts

Complicated situations may arise when deciding whether to accept certain gifts, and they should be considered carefully. Here are two examples:

- *A donor offers an endowed chair in an area that is not related to mission and in which the institution has no expertise, no faculty, no resources, and no students.* Funding for an endowed chair in a brand-new area very likely will not pay the full cost of a new professor or provide additional library, laboratory, or staff resources unless there is a government or private source for matching funds. Unless the chair will establish a program that is part of the institution's strategic plan, the gift should be rejected. If the offer does fulfill a need, the president can decide whether to accept the financial burden.

- *A donor offers a significant gift, but he wants his late wife's name on all four sides of an existing building in letters far larger than those used on other signage throughout the campus.* A gift that undermines the integrity of the campus signage and design is not worth having.

Many gifts add to the expense side of the budget even though they may produce some revenue. Boards and presidents should be cautious that fundraising does not add to the institution's financial burdens in ways that are inconsistent with the strategic plan or institutional mission. They will have to decide which needs are so pressing that it may be worth the cost to accept gifts that provide only partial funding.

The president and board have the most flexibility to achieve goals and meet needs when a gift is unrestricted and liquid (for example, cash) and the least flexibility when a gift is restricted to a particular purpose and illiquid (such as property or equipment). The best gift of all is one from a donor who tells the president to use the money for the institution's greatest need. This situation is rare, but it happens.

Early in the Rollins campaign, I received a call from an alumnus whose interests were almost exclusively athletics-based. However, I knew his wife, an alumna, had majored in English, and I wanted to establish a chair in that department. The alumnus did not object, and his gift established an emphasis on faculty chairs throughout the campaign.

Ethical Challenges

There is nothing more important than the good reputation of an institution and its leaders. Once lost, public trust is difficult to regain.

The preservation of a good reputation depends, in large measure, on a commitment to ethical behavior in every dimension of institutional life. Ethical leadership is arguably most vital in the fundraising area because it links an institution's commitment to ethical behavior with trust in donor relationships.

> **The best gifts are those from a donor who tells the president to use the money for the institution's greatest need. This situation is rare, but it happens.**

Preservation of a good reputation depends, in large measure, on a commitment to ethical behavior in every dimension of institutional life. Ethical leadership is arguably most vital in the fundraising area because it links an institution's commitment to ethical behavior with trust in donor relationships.

The president is the institution's chief ethical standard bearer and must be beyond reproach in speech and behavior. A lapse at the top gives constituents the impression that any behavior is acceptable. The president and chief development officer should work with the board to incorporate ethical standards in fundraising and campaign policies. CASE and other fundraising organizations offer sample statements of ethics, and sample donor bills of rights are also available. The full board should discuss and approve fundraising standards and policies. However, policy statements are not sufficient. To really understand and internalize what is acceptable and what is not, it is useful for board members, volunteers, senior administrators, and development staff members to review and discuss these policies annually.

Discussion of case examples is especially helpful. There are numerous sources of cases dealing with ethics, but faculty or staff members can also create them based on their experiences. There are many subtle interactions with ethical implications that can be confusing to people. An ethics professor may be able to develop case studies and lead discussions on ethics in fundraising.

Clear policies would guide staff in handling the following ethical dilemmas:

- *A board member asks a development staff member for a research file containing personal information about a donor.* The prospect information gleaned from publicly available materials can be shared, but personal information should be protected. It helps if the institution's written policy makes this clear. While it is difficult to deny access to a board member, the president or board chair can intervene.

- *A major donor seeks preferential treatment in admissions, employment, or business for a relative or friend.* Admissions, employment, and business decisions must be completely separate from fundraising interests. Once the integrity of these processes is compromised, there is a slippery slope to more and more inappropriate and unethical behavior.

- *A donor leaves a bequest of a valuable painting to the planned giving officer who has admired it in the past.* Though many donors develop close relationships with institutional representatives, under no circumstances is it appropriate to accept valuable personal gifts or bequests from donors. Gift-acceptance policies, conflict-of-interest policies, and codes of ethics and business practices must be clear in defining how to avoid these awkward situations.

Leaders can protect the institution's reputation by discussing, promoting, and modeling ethical behavior. It is the responsibility of presidents, CDOs, and board members to hold themselves and others to the highest ethical standards.

Does "Tainted" Money Taint an Institution?

In the early part of the 20th century, transformational gifts were offered by donors known as "robber barons" (Andrew Carnegie, John D. Rockefeller, Henry Ford, and others)—men who built great power and wealth through questionable business practices. Their generosity was thought to be a way of securing social approbation and redemption.[21] The tainted-money question is not simple. Most colleges and universities do not wish to be associated with donors who are found to have been involved in illegal or unethical behaviors. In some cases, an institution has named a facility, a program, an endowed chair, or a scholarship fund for a donor who was later convicted of a crime. A number of institutions in this position have

Donors who have less-than-stellar reputations may try to improve their status by investing in a visible project. Boards and presidents need to decide whether to facilitate such a reputational rehabilitation.

removed the donor's name, and some have returned the money.

A more subtle and challenging decision is whether to provide visibility for donors who have a reputation for unethical although not illegal behavior. Donors who have less-than-stellar reputations may try to improve their status by investing in a visible project. Boards and presidents need to decide whether to facilitate such a reputational rehabilitation.

In the 1980s, Harvard University decided to divest itself of a large portfolio of stocks and bonds in Exxon Corporation and other oil companies because they were doing business in South Africa under the apartheid system. Harvard's leaders did not believe that the decision should also have prevented them from accepting funds from the Exxon Educational Foundation. But foundation president Robert L. Payton felt that if holding the company's stock was morally unacceptable, accepting gifts from the same source should also be unacceptable.[22]

At another institution, the administration declined to accept a gift from an individual with a negative reputation who wanted his name on a building visible from the highway. At another, the board voted to rename a dormitory that for years had carried the name of an avowed Ku Klux Klan organizer.

On occasion, institutions receive support from donors who later go to prison for financial abuses. Such was the case with Bernard Madoff, who was on the board investment committees of several universities. Rollins was the victim in a similar case, in which Tom Petters, a board member who had pledged millions of dollars to the college, received a federal prison term for a Ponzi scheme.

There are no clear guidelines to address such vexing issues, and each institution must establish its own practices. Institutions must protect their reputations and set a high standard for ethical behavior. They should not besmirch the institution's good name by associating it with an unsavory donor, no matter how much money is involved.

There are other views on the matter, however. One long-serving president, who led an underendowed institution, used to say that he kept a washing machine outside his door that cleaned up any "dirty" money, which he could then put to good use.

In 2011, the UCLA School of Law announced a $10-million gift to establish a business law institute. The gift was from Lowell Milken who, with his older brother Michael, played a role in creating the junk-bond market in the 1980s. Michael went to prison, but in a deal, charges against Lowell were dropped. This gift caused dissension among the faculty. Some argued that accepting it would damage the reputations of the law school and its faculty, while others were grateful for the donor's generosity, especially in light of state cuts to higher education.[23]

Board members, presidents, senior administrators, faculty members, and development professionals should all be involved in thinking through the ethics and the consequences of taking money that may be tainted and providing clarification through relevant policies.

Keeping Faith with Donors

One of the cardinal rules of fundraising, and a basic matter of ethics, is to faithfully follow donor intentions and institutional commitments for the use and naming of gifts. Universities and colleges have angered donors by selling donated paintings, radio stations, and other property, as well as by using dedicated endowment funds for purposes other than originally planned. When agreements are abrogated, there may be legal ramifications.

Princeton University, for example, had a long-running dispute with the Robertson family about the way in which a 1961 gift had been applied. The university settled the dispute by paying $50 million to the heirs' foundation and about that much in legal fees.

Before accepting gifts, presidents must be certain that the institution can and will abide by the donor's intent or the gifts should not be accepted. Otherwise, the institution will also develop a reputation for mismanaging gifts and being untrustworthy that inevitably dampens future giving.

While colleges and universities must honor donor intent, they cannot allow donors to have control over the disposition of their gift: The Internal Revenue Service disallows donations as gifts if the donor is given too much influence in the application of those gifts. So, for example, donors cannot select the professors who will hold their endowed chairs or the students who will receive their scholarship funds.

In the spring of 2011, the new president of Florida State University faced criticism for a gift of $1.5 million accepted by his predecessor. The gift was to develop new curricula and establish new positions in the economics department. However, in return for the gift, the donor was given the right to set up a committee to decide which candidates to consider. A petition with 9,000 signatures was sent to the president asking him to terminate the agreement, which was probably legally as well as ethically wrong. The agreement was changed.

One simple yet vital habit that reflects well on the institution, pleases donors, and encourages others to give is always to use the appropriate name when referring to a donor-supported facility, chair, program, or scholarship. This practice enhances a culture of philanthropy and reminds all constituents of the contributions of philanthropy to the work of the institution.

On occasion, a donor requests anonymity. Such a request must be honored, but the president or chief development officer should raise several issues: Would the donor reconsider and allow the institution to publicize the gift as a spur to other giving? Is the gift to remain anonymous in perpetuity? Are there any board members, administrators, or potential donors who can be told?

Donors may also be susceptible to the suggestions and guidance of the staff and president. It is vital to be extremely careful to recommend only actions that are good for the individual as well as for the institution. Institutional representatives can seek to influence donors ethically, which means putting donor interests first.

One generous donor mentioned periodically to the president of his alma mater that his advisors were urging him to establish a foundation. He had no children or close relatives. When the subject arose, the president pointed out to him that when he, his trust officer, lawyer, and investment banker were gone, people he did not know would be distributing his money. This donor listened to the president and never established a foundation. As a result, when he died his alma mater received more than $100 million. His generosity transformed the small college, while a foundation would likely have spread the funds over a variety of institutions without changing any of them significantly.

In this situation, the donor was pleased with his ability to make a bequest that would transform his alma mater. The president felt no regrets at exerting her personal influence to secure the future of the college without undermining the donor's best interests. This case illustrates the obligation of presidents to understand and support the best interests of donors and to provide considered advice when warranted.

TIPS

FOR PRESIDENTS

- In fundraising, as in all aspects of university life, the president and board must demonstrate the most exemplary ethical behavior. Once an institution betrays the public trust, it is extraordinarily difficult to regain it. Policies and procedures covering all aspects of advancement should be in place and reviewed annually with staff members, administrators, and board members.

- Adhere faithfully to agreements between a donor and the institution regarding the purpose of a gift, donor recognition, and naming. On rare occasions, such agreements are no longer viable for the institution. If the issue cannot be resolved, the institution may have to go to court to seek approval for changes.

- Consider each gift with care and thought, and do not automatically accept every gift that is offered. Gifts that have strings attached, require too much cost to the institution, enable excessive donor involvement, or are meant for the rehabilitation of a donor's reputation may need to be redirected or declined diplomatically.

- Employees of the institution should decline personal gifts from donors, contractors, or suppliers. Such relationships are based on connections made through the institution and are not typical friendships. Acceptance of personal gifts is viewed as a conflict of interest.

Conclusion
Planning for the Long Term

You have to do a lot of educating and hope that you'll be capable of convincing people that the university's priorities should be taken seriously. ... [On] the whole I have found that not to be forbiddingly difficult.[24]

Gerhard Casper, President Emeritus, Stanford University

THE ROLE OF THE PRESIDENT AND THE BOARD to protect and enhance an institution's financial health, academic quality, and reputation has become especially challenging as government resources dwindle, student populations require increased remedial work and financing, and the economy remains weak. These trends do not show signs of immediate reversal, so there is considerable pressure on presidents and boards to augment institutional resources. Some colleges and universities use endowment funds to buy property and build facilities, a practice that should be followed cautiously and infrequently. Decisions such as deferring maintenance, accepting inadequate technology backup systems, or increasing the percentage of contingent (part-time) faculty may have short-term financial benefits but also grave implications for both the current and future health of the institution.

Although philanthropy alone will not solve all the problems of a university or college, presidents, with the active engagement of their boards and support of a highly motivated development staff, can secure the financial resources that will strengthen their institutions while protecting the endowment for future generations of students.

Presidential Transitions

The retirement or departure of a president can have a substantial impact on current and future fundraising. When presidents leave after a significant tenure character- ized by successful fundraising, thoughtful consideration should be given to ways of maintaining their connections with key donors without undermining the ability of the new president to develop her or his own relationships. This is a challenge, but it is important to donors to whom the outgoing president has served as a friend and trusted leader for many years. Severing those relationships precipitously may give rise to the belief that the outgoing president's attentions have been solely about money. This also holds true for the chief development officer.

When I left the University of Miami, I left behind many friendships I had made with donors. I made no phone calls, sent no letters, and did not visit. In short, I lost

When presidents leave after a significant tenure characterized by successful fundraising, thoughtful consideration should be given to ways of maintaining their connections with key donors without undermining the ability of the new president to develop her or his own relationships.

Fundraising prowess is a major litmus test by which a president is judged and remembered. Without sufficient resources, little progress can be achieved toward academic, faculty, or student quality.

all contact with them. I had gotten busy at Rollins, but, if I had been asked, I would happily have made contact. Later, I heard that one generous woman said, "I guess she was only after my money." I was very fond of her, so that was painful to hear and not true. When I departed Rollins College, I again severed ties with donors, as I thought it best to avoid initiating such contacts. I now believe that a thoughtful plan for donor relations could have eased the transitions in both institutions.

A number of institutions intentionally plan a period during which one president gradually hands off contacts to another. The board, too, can play an important role in ensuring that the transition is smooth and relationships with donors are maintained. On the other hand, if a president leaves under a cloud, fundraising will suffer as constituents express concern about the lack of board oversight, the probity of the administration, and the health of the institution. Under such circumstances, it is up to the development office to ensure that connections with prospects are maintained until a new president is installed.

During a time of transition, board members can help take up the slack and spend extra time on campus and with donors. For the health of the institution, there needs to be continuity in these relationships.

Will You Still Love Me Tomorrow?

The job of a president and a board is to leave the institution in better shape than when he or she took office; to strengthen its academic quality, financial health, and reputation; to ensure current and future students a good education; and to respond to the needs of its community as best it can.

When presidents leave an institution, they look back with pride on important contributions they made to improved academic quality, strengthened standards for tenure and promotion, increased application and graduation rates, increased student selectivity, and curriculum revisions. They are often best remembered, however, for the money they raised to construct buildings, increase the endowment, and strengthen the institution's financial health.

Fundraising prowess is a major litmus test by which a president is judged and remembered. Without sufficient resources, little progress can be achieved toward academic, faculty, or student quality. The work of the president is interconnected, and a focus on both mission and resources is vital. Being driven by mission alone is fruitless; resources without a compelling mission are easily squandered or misdirected.

Presidents who understand how to integrate the full range of job requirements—academic leadership, student life, financial management, constituent relations, policy advocacy, fundraising—can ensure a positive legacy. Presidents who integrate those activities and collaborate with board members and faculty members in the process will leave a positive and lasting imprint on the institution. And, by the time their presidency concludes, the work of fundraising will have become less stressful, more pleasurable, and more successful.

Presidents who understand how to integrate the full range of job requirements—academic leadership, student life, financial management, constituent relations, policy advocacy, fundraising—can ensure a positive legacy. . . . And, by the time their presidency concludes, the work of fundraising will have become less stressful, more pleasurable, and more successful.

NOTES

[1] Peter T. Flawn, *A Primer for University Presidents: Managing the Modern University* (Austin: University of Texas Press, 1990), p. 174.

[2] Merle Curti and Roderick Nash, *Philanthropy and the Shaping of American Higher Education* (New Brunswick, NJ: Rutgers University Press, 1965), p. 55.

[3] Jeffrey Selingo, "Leaders' Views About Higher Education, Their Jobs, and Their Lives," The *Chronicle of Higher Education*, November 5, 2005. http://chronicle.com/article/Leaders-Views-About-Higher/22369.

[4] Quoted in Rita Bornstein, *Legitimacy in the Academic Presidency: From Entrance to Exit* (Westport, CT: American Council on Education and Praeger, 2003), p. 124.

[5] AGB Task Force on the State of the Presidency in American Higher Education, *The Leadership Imperative* (Washington, DC: Association of Governing Boards, 2006).

[6] Quoted in Robert Birnbaum, *Speaking of Higher Education: The Academic's Book of Quotations* (Westport, CT: American Council on Education/Praeger, 2004), p. 203.

[7] Quoted in Frank H. T. Rhodes, ed., *Successful Fund Raising for Higher Education* (Washington, D.C.: American Council on Education and Oryx Press, 1997), p. 98.

[8] Lonnie Ostrom, Paul W. Fombelle, Eugene R. Tempel, and James Ward, "Matching Willingness to Can Do: Enhancing the President's Role in Higher Education Fundraising," unpublished article (2011), pp. 3–4.

[9] Arthur Levine, *Higher Learning in America, 1980–2000* (Baltimore: Johns Hopkins University Press, 1993), p. 195.

[10] Ostrom et al., 2011, p. 10.

[11] Quoted in Bornstein, *Legitimacy in the Academic Presidency*, p. 128.

[12] Jerald Panas, *Mega Gifts: Who Gives Them, Who Gets Them* (Chicago: Pluribus Press, 1984), p. 185.

[13] Paul G. Schervish and John J. Havens, *Millionaires and the Millennium: Prospects for a Golden Age of Philanthropy* (Boston: Social Welfare Research Institute, Boston College, 1999); Schervish, "Today's Wealth Holder and Tomorrow's Giving: The New Dynamics of Wealth and Philanthropy," *Journal of Gift Planning* 9, no. 3 (2005): 15–37.

[14] Frank H. T. Rhodes, ed., *Successful Fund-Raising for Higher Education: The Advancement of Learning* (Phoenix, AZ: American Council on Education and Oryx Press, 1997), p. xxiv.

[15] Quoted in Eugene R. Tempel, Timothy L. Seiler, and Eva E. Aldrich, *Achieving Excellence in Fundraising* (San Francisco: Jossey-Bass, 2011), p. 4.

[16] Sherri Welch, "The Color of Philanthropy: Black Donors Often Under the Radar," *Crain's Detroit Business*, May 8, 2011.

[17] Quoted in Frank H. T. Rhodes, ed., *Successful Fund Raising for Higher Education: The Advancement of Learning* (Phoenix, AZ: American Council on Education/Oryx Press, 1997), p. 36.

[18] *CASE Reporting Standards and Management Guidelines for Educational Fundraising*, 4th ed. (Washington, D.C.: CASE, 2009); CASE Campaign Report 2010 (Washington, DC: CASE, 2011).

[19] Andrea Fuller, "Updates on Capital Campaigns at 36 Colleges and Universities," The *Chronicle of Higher Education*, November 21, 2010. http://chronicle.com/article/Updates-on-Capital-Campaigns/125455/

[20] Jill Ker Conway, *A Woman's Education* (New York: Knopf, 2001), p. 66.

[21] Barry D. Karl and Stanley N. Katz, "Foundations and Ruling Class Elites," *Daedalus* 116, no. 1 (Winter 1987): 1–4.

[22] Robert Payton, "Tainted Money: The Ethics and Rhetoric of Divestment," *Change: The Magazine of Higher Learning*, May-June 1987, pp. 55–60.

[23] Julie Creswell and Peter Lattman, "Milken Gift Stirs Dispute at UCLA," *The New York Times*, August 23, 2011.

[24] Quoted in Henry Muller, "I Have At Least Nine Jobs," interview with Gerhard Casper, *Fortune* online, October 16, 2000.

ADDITIONAL RESOURCES

David Bass, "College Fundraising: Is There a 'New Normal?'" *Trusteeship*, November/December 2009.

Julie Bourbon, "What Does the Economy Bode for Fundraising?" *Trusteeship*, November/December 2008.

John T. Casteen III, "Financial Self-Sufficiency and the Public University." *Trusteeship*, May/June 2011.

Gary Evans, *Development Committee* (Washington, DC: Association of Governing Boards of Universities and Colleges, 2003).

Richard D. Legon, *The Board's Role in Fund-Raising* (Washington, DC: Association of Governing Boards of Universities and Colleges, 2003).

Jake B. Schrum, ed., *A Board's Guide to Comprehensive Campaigns* (Washington, DC: Association of Governing Boards of Universities and Colleges, 2000).

Michael J. Worth, *Securing the Future: A Fundraising Guide for Boards of Independent Colleges and Universities* (Washington, DC: Association of Governing Boards of Universities and Colleges, 2005).

Michael J. Worth, *Sounding Boards: Advisory Councils in Higher Education* (Washington, DC: Association of Governing Boards of Universities and Colleges, 2008).

About the Author

Rita Bornstein is president emerita and Cornell Professor of Philanthropy and Leadership Development at Rollins College, where she was president from 1990 to 2004. Previously, she was vice president for development at the University of Miami. She serves on the boards of the Association of Governing Boards of Universities and Colleges, Tupperware Corporation, and the Dr. P. Philips Orlando Performing Arts Center. Dr. Bornstein has received numerous awards and three honorary doctorates. She consults, speaks, and writes on issues related to leadership, governance, and fundraising and is frequently quoted in articles on higher education governance and leadership. Her books include *Legitimacy in the Academic Presidency: From Entrance to Exit* (ACE/Greenwood Press, 2003) and *Succession Planning for the Higher Education Presidency* (AGB Press, 2010).